Making Money with

Funds

Samuel Blankson

ISBN: 1-4116-2671-0

Acknowledgements

Thanks to God for filling my cup to overflowing and guiding me through the valley of the shadow of death. Thanks to my wonderful wife Uju for making the journey fun and always being there for me, and finally to Chuck Mellon, Tom McCarthy, Tony Robbins, leaders of the Amway Corporation and the Yager Organisation for teaching, training and guiding me in the early days.

Contents

Introduction

Today the world fund market is a multi trillion-dollar industry. There are many types of funds and as many reasons for choosing them. In this book, you will learn how Funds work, and how you can profitably trade them.

Samuel Blankson

Chapter 1

- *What are Funds*

What is a fund?

When a group of investors pool their funds together, hire a manager to oversee, allocate, and trade this fund in equities (stocks and shares), debt (bonds, fixed income), and other securities (other funds, REITS etc), as well as redistributing interest, dividends, and other profits back to investors, a fund is born. Sometimes investors do not initiate this fund, a financial institution will decide to start a fund and thus seek to attract money from investors into the fund.

Whichever way it begins, all funds have the same objective. This objective is primarily to make money for the fund manager and hopefully to make the investor money too.

There are many types of funds available to suit all types of investors. Many ways have been devised to charge investors commission, management fees, and transaction fees for the privilege of being a fund member.

Whole industries have sprung up to feed on these funds. From government taxes, to broker loading fees (mainly referral-based commissions).

To invest successfully in funds, seek to avoid these charges, and select funds that offer you low risks with high gains.

What Are The Different Fund Types And Their Characteristics?

There are two main types of funds:

1. *Open-Ended Funds.* They sell as many shares as investors wish to buy. They also buy back as many shares as investors wish to sell. (The majority of mutual funds in the US and unit trusts in the UK are open-ended).
2. *Closed-Ended Funds or Investment Trusts (also called Investments Funds).* Investment trusts have a fixed number of stocks. They are traded like shares, and are regulated by the Investment Company Act of 1940 (see *http://www.law.uc.edu/CCL/InvCoAct*).

Open-Ended Funds

An open-ended fund has an unlimited amount of units to sell. Each unit it sells reduces the NAV. The NAV is the Net Asset Value of the fund, divided by the total amount of units held by investors. An investor wishing to buy shares in the fund would pay the NAV per unit.

The underlying asset value changes because the shares, bonds, and other securities prices change. The amount of units sold also changes, and so the NAV changes. Therefore, at any moment in a high volume fund, the unit price will be moving. When you come to sell your units, you will receive the current NAV per unit.

This can be confusing so let us look at a simple example:

Open-Ended Fund X (at time of purchase)
Current units = 100,000
Underlying assets value = $1,000,000
Current NAV = $10

If you had $1000 to invest in Fund X, you would get 100 units, each worth $10 at time of purchase.

Because the underlying assets all pay interest (bonds) or dividends (equity), most open-ended funds are setup to reinvest these payments by buying more units, automatically.

Let us then say that a year later you want to sell your units. During the interim, the underlying assets have paid dividends and interest that amounted to 10 more units (remember these are reinvested). Therefore, you now have 110 units.

Let us also suppose that the underlying assets have increased in value by 10% in the interim. Therefore, the new picture is as follows:

Open-Ended Fund X (one year later)
Current units = 110,000. (Let us assume no new units were sold, and all unit dividends and interests were reinvested into more units. Let us also assume that there were no redemption charges levied in the interim).

Underlying assets value = $1,100,000
Current NAV = $10

You have 110 units so you would receive $1100 for your units. This would be a 10% increase in this simple example.

That is how open-ended funds work.

There is an overwhelming amount of open-ended funds to choose from; therefore, they are liquid and flexible. Their popularity has grown greatly in the last 20 years, almost to the same levels as their underlying equity. In the US, there is an open-ended fund investor to account for each household

We will revisit this fund type again shortly. In the mean time, let us look at the closed-ended fund.

Closed-Ended Funds

Closed-ended funds raise money from the public by offering a limited number of units for sale. When these units are all sold, the fund is closed. From then onwards, to buy these units, investors have to go to the stock exchange and hope someone is willing to sell. If some of the original investors want to sell their units, they also have to do so via the stock exchanges.

Because the values of these units are due to supply and demand, the price will not be a reflection of the NAV. Instead, the traded price is often 30% below NAV. With closed-ended funds, there is less to choose from, therefore, they are inflexible and illiquid. These simple facts have driven closed-ended funds almost into obscurity in comparison to open-ended funds. Today they are used mainly by institutional investors and other sophisticated investors.

How to Trade Funds Successfully

We shall now look at how to make money with funds. We will concentrate on open-ended funds for obvious reasons.

There are four main ways to make money with funds, these are:

1. Dividends on stocks and interest on bonds. This type of payment is called a distribution. Funds distribute almost all earned income from the underlying assets.
2. When a fund liquidates some of its assets, there could be a possibility for investors to receive further distributions if the assets value has appreciated, and if the fund has a policy of passing on these gains to investors.

3. Funds are traded on stock market exchanges. If an underlying asset increases in value and the fund does not liquidate it, the market price of the fund will also appreciate in value allowing you to be able to profit by selling your shares in the fund on the exchange.
4. Most funds give their investors the option of reinvesting distributions back into the fund.

Today the most popular fund types are mutual funds. (These are known as unit trusts in the UK, although a unit trust is not technically a mutual fund, but it behaves the same way).

We will concentrate specifically on open–ended mutual funds. Open-ended mutual funds have several advantages and it is important to understand these advantages so that you can better determine when to use them.

Advantages of mutual funds:

1. ***Professional Management*** - Funds employ qualified professional traders who manage the fund. This advantage is oversold because looking at some funds performance; you would not think professional fund managers managed them. After reading this book and applying its investment strategies, you will be able to beat the performance of most funds.
2. ***Diversification*** – Funds pool millions, often billions, of dollar buying power into their underlying assets. This allows the fund to diversify in many equities and debt instruments. This is something that you would not be able to do as effectively, given your available funds.
3. ***Buying power*** – The huge buying power of funds allows them to reduce their transaction costs. The resultant negligible transaction costs further increase the fund's efficiency and profitability.

4. ***Liquidity*** - As we saw in the explanation for open-ended funds, the unlimited amount of units makes mutual funds exceptionally liquid. You can buy and sell them at any moment during the exchange trading hours. (Some unethical individuals even do so after the exchange closes, making it look as if they traded during trading hours).

5. ***Ease of Acquisition*** – Mutual funds are easy to purchase and have low minimum purchase size requirements. There are now many regular payment plans offered by banks and financial institutions that will allow you to invest from $50 per month into mutual funds.

Disadvantages of mutual funds:

1. ***Professional Management*** – Because most managers are paid regardless of the funds performance, they are not greatly motivated to perform well. Another thing that happens is certain managers are better in a particular economic cycle than others. Often you will see a fund performing well during a bull market, whilst it will loose value during a Bear market. It is easy for most traders to make money when the going is good; the true test of a great trader is how they perform during the bad times.

2. ***Costs*** – The real ingenuity in mutual funds lies in their costing systems. Never has a financial instrument been devised that so efficiently ebbs at your profits through fees and charges. More will be covered on this later on page 19.

3. ***Dilution*** – When you over diversify, you loose the effect of movement in either direction. This is because each asset is such a minority of the whole, that its appreciation or depreciation in value, no matter how great, will not make a major impact on the portfolio as a whole. This can happen to funds

that invest in too many assets or in a fund of funds (a fund that invest in other funds).

4. ***Taxes*** – When investing in assets yourself, you can defer taxes to a future date to better suit your situation. However, when you invest into a fund, you no longer control this. If the fund liquidates an asset whose value has appreciated, you will be liable to pay capital gains tax on that distribution.

Today, the amount of mutual funds available exceeds stocks; this is great news for the mutual fund investor. With so many funds available, there is bound to be one to suit every investor's style and preference. That means different risk levels and returns are available to the investor. However, selecting the right one can be a daunting task if you had to review them all individually. Luckily, for us, there are fund screeners that automate most of this task. This will be covered in more detail later.

Mutual funds are similar in many ways but also different in some fundamental ways. The type of assets a fund invests in, and the strategies it uses, are two of these defining fundamentals. Let us look at these differences in detail.

There are three main types of mutual fund, they are:

1. ***Money market funds*** – These are the safest mutual funds available.
   a. *Treasury Bills*: These are short-term government debt.
   b. *Certificates of Deposit (CD)*: These offer a higher yield than treasure bills, and pay dividends monthly, semi-annually or annually. A CD is a deposit at a bank for a specific term. During that term, you will be paid interest. The period of interest payments will determine the effectiveness of the CD, with the shortest periods generating

the most yields. These are offered in any denomination and range from three months to five-year maturity terms.

c. *Commercial Paper*: This is a loan to a corporation for one to nine months. The denominations are normally from $100,000 upwards. The corporations that issue these normally have very high credit ratings. They are normally issued at a discount.

d. *Bankers Acceptance*: This is a short-term credit issued by a company and guaranteed by a bank. They do not need to be held onto until maturity, as they are traded in the secondary markets. They are normally issued at a discount.

e. *Eurodollars*: This is a US dollar denominated deposit in banks outside the US. They are sold at narrow margins due to regulation-free trade outside the US. They are normally for millions of dollars.

f. *Repos*: These are repurchase agreements normally held from overnight to 30 days or more. This is the selling of treasury bills and repurchasing them for an agreed price, at an agreed date. There are two variations on the standard repo, which are as follows:

- Standard repo.
- Term repo – this is a repo where the term is over 30 days.
- Reverse repo – this is a repo where the dealer buys a treasury bill from an investor and sells it back for a higher price later.

2. ***Fixed-income funds***
   a. *Government bond funds*: These invest in government debt securities. In the US, these invest in treasury bills, treasury notes, treasury bonds, and mortgage-backed securities issued by

government lending agencies such as Fannie Mae. Some bond funds are exempt from federal tax. They are some of the safest funds you can invest in; however, their returns are quite low. Their main risk is related to fluctuating interest rates and inflation.

b. *Municipal bond funds*: These invest in state and local government issued debt securities. These bond funds are exempt from federal taxes, and in some cases, from state taxes too.

c. *Corporate bond funds*: These invest in corporate debt. The underlying bond could default if companies that issue them go bankrupt.

d. *Zero-coupon bond funds*: These invest in zero coupon bonds.

e. *International bond funds*: These invest in bonds issued by foreign governments and corporations.

f. *Convertible securities funds*: These invest in bonds that may be converted into stock.

g. *Multi-sector bond funds*: These invest in all types of bonds: corporate bonds, municipal bonds, international bonds etc.

3. **Equity Funds**

a. *Growth funds*: These invest in stocks with the potential for long-term capital appreciation, keeping their focus on companies experiencing earnings and revenue growth. These funds are great in bull markets but often fall further than other funds in bear markets.

b. *Value funds*: These invest in companies that appear to have good fundamentals, and are trading at low P/E (price to earnings) ratios. They tend to pay high dividends, as their value is higher than their price.

c. *Aggressive growth funds*: These invest in companies that are experiencing rapid growth.

These funds are highly risky as they take more risks and trade more frequently. They may invest in IPOs, options, and futures. These are all very high-risk investments.

d. *Blended funds*: These invest in both value and growth stocks to capitalise on current income and long-term capital appreciation within the same fund.

e. *Sector funds:* These invest in a single sector of the market. These funds are good to use as a growth fund to cover a sector that is experiencing rapid growth or is poised to do so.

f. *Large Cap, Mid Cap, Small Cap, and Micro Cap funds*: They invest primarily in stocks that match the capitalisation criteria. Normally, the smaller the cap, the more volatile and risky the fund.

g. *Focused funds*: These invest primarily in a small number of stocks. Their emphasis is on quality not quantity, and they can hold as few as 10 stocks.

h. *Index funds*: These invest in stocks to mirror an index. They do not require active management, as their stock selection is automatic. They are passively managed, with their main advantages being lower management fees, lower transaction costs, and therefore, lower capital gains tax. (Every time an asset is liquidated at profit, you have to pay capital gains tax on the profits. Most indexes do not change their stocks frequently; therefore, their investors have less need to pay taxes).

i. *Exchange-Traded Funds (ETFs)*: This is a financial instrument that creates a portfolio of securities using a trust (a legal entity much like a company), and trades the portfolio on a stock exchange. You can then buy shares in the portfolio. ETFs only buy securities that offer real time holdings disclosure; therefore, actively managed mutual funds are not included in the portfolio. Because of its status as a company, the ETF stocks can be treated in every way as you would a normal company stock. This includes short selling. There is an ETF for most major indexes like the SPDR for the S&P 500, QQQQ for the NASDAQ 100 and DIA for the Dow Jones Industrial Average.

Chapter 2

- *Understanding The Personalities Of Funds*

Understanding the Personalities of Funds

There are many flavours of mutual funds. However, the vast majority are equity funds. MorningStar popularised the fund style box (see http://news.MorningStar.com/news/Ms/Investing101/stylebox.html); this style box can be used to categorise the style of a fund. MorningStar's professional analysts rate these funds, giving them a risk rating, and placing them in a box within their famous style box. For a list of ETFs with style boxes, see Appendix 2.

You can read all about the style box from MorningStar's website provided above. When looking at MorningStar's style box, keep in mind that for lower risk, stick with funds with a rating in the top left hand corner, and for higher risk, stick with funds with a rating in the opposite corner (bottom right hand corner).

Morningstar's Rating System

Lets look a little closer at the rating system used by most of the fund industry, the MorningStar system (see *http://news.MorningStar.com/news/Ms/Investing101/stylebox.ht ml* for more details).

Value rating refers to stocks with good fundamentals but that are currently under priced. This is a long-term style.

Growth is a style that invests in stocks that are growing fast, and may be over priced.

Blend refers to a compromise of growth and value.

Size ratings refer to the stock's market capitalisation. With Large representing the top 5% of equities, Mid representing the next 15% after Large, and Small representing the bottom 80%.

Once you understand this system of rating and analysing of a fund, you can go to *http://www.mfea.com/FundSelector* where you can screen funds for your preferred style, and risk level.

To complete the list of fund types, here are the rest of the available fund types:

1. ***Income Funds***: These invest in fixed income producing securities. These securities could include high dividend paying preferred stock, bonds, and government securities. These funds are great at producing a steady income.
2. ***Asset Allocation Funds***: These invest in a number of different asset classes, such as stocks, bonds, and cash to achieve asset allocation goals. These are different from blended/balanced funds because they invest in more asset classes than the latter.
3. ***Global Funds***: These invest in assets spread all over the globe to achieve their diversification goals. These funds introduce other risks, i.e. currency fluctuations and political and/or economic instability.
4. ***International/Foreign Funds***: These invest in all but domestic assets. As with global funds, international funds are at risk from political, economic, currency instability and fluctuations.
5. ***Regional Funds***: These invest internationally but in only one region, i.e. Far East, Middle East etc.
6. ***Emerging Markets Funds***: These invest only in markets, which are going through a major economic transition (i.e. third world countries moving from agricultural to industrial economies). These are very risky as the transition could fail and the currencies are very volatile.
7. ***Mortgage-Backed Securities Funds***: These invest in home mortgage securities that are offered through several government agencies. In the US, these are

Ginnie Mae - Government National Mortgage Association (GNMA), Fannie Mae - Federal National Mortgage Association (FNMA), and Freddie Mac - Federal Home Loan Mortgage Corp (FHLMC). These agencies purchase and then pool together groups of home mortgage loans, reselling them later to mutual funds and other investors as a single security. These funds earn interest on mortgages. These interests are passed on to shareholders, as well as principal payments, which they use to reinvest into more securities. These securities are considered very secure, as they are national government or federal government backed. However, they could be settled earlier or loose interest due to falling interest rates.

8. ***Hedge Funds***: These invest in derivatives; use short selling and large margins (loans) to create leverage. They can do this because they are exempt from many restrictive rules governing other funds. One of their restrictions however, is a limit on investors. They are only allowed 100 investors per fund. For this reason they require high minimal investments from investors (from $10,000 although the average is over $100,000). Hedge funds collect a percentage of all profits earned (normally 20%).

9. ***Fund Supermarkets***: These allow investors to buy funds from mutual fund families, therefore simplifying their statements, and accounting. This method is also a convenient way to access many products from the same family of funds. All other benefits of these types of funds are only marketing talk, because they have hidden charges that make them as expensive (fees and charges) as most other funds not in the family of funds.

10. ***Fund of Funds (FOFs)***: These invest in other mutual funds. They have two major drawbacks. Firstly, they compound the costs of all the funds they invest in,

and secondly, they duplicate securities, giving a non-accurate diversification measure.

11. *Lifecycle Funds*: These funds attempt to perform the asset allocation portfolio distribution for the three major roles of your life, namely youth, middle age, and retirement age. They do this by shifting investment strategy through the years from growth to blended, then finally to value.

12. *Institutional Funds*: These invest in hundreds of different securities to create some of the most diversified funds available. They aim to attract pension funds, endowments, and high net worth investors. They can be purchased for $1,000-$5,000, and offer great savings in transaction costs due to low transaction activity.

13. *Socially Responsible Funds*: These invest in ethical, moral, and environmentally sound companies. These funds try to achieve high returns within their guiding principles.

14. *Contrarian Funds*: These invest in the opposite direction of the prevailing market sentiment. During bear markets, they invest in bullish securities and visa versa. Because of these limits, contrarian funds only tend to do well during market transitions.

15. *Guaranteed Investment Contracts (GIC) Funds*: These invest solely in Guaranteed Investment Contracts (GICs). GICs are fixed income debt issued by insurance companies. They pay a fixed interest rate over the term (normally within five years). These securities are mainly bought by pension and retirement plan funds. The guarantor is the insurance company.

16. *Unit Investment Trusts (UITs)*: This closed-ended fund operates as a mutual fund until the initial offering stocks are all sold. There are three disadvantages to UITs. Firstly, you can only purchase them from the issuing investment house. Secondly, you

cannot easily get pricing information on them for research purposes before you buy. Finally, they have restrictively high entry and exit fees. The sole benefit of UITs is their low transaction and maintenance fees.

17. *Market Neutral Funds*: These invest in long and short-term securities in an attempt to eliminate risk. However, they use leveraging to achieve higher than treasury bill returns.

18. *Option and Futures Funds*: These invest in options and futures. These are the most risky funds available. They do not own any underlying security. Instead, they have the right or obligation to purchase these underlying securities at a fixed future date. These funds are only advised for the experienced investor. (See *The Practical Guide to Total Financial Freedom: Volume 4*, for a fuller explanation of options and futures).

Mutual Fund Fees

Mutual fund fees can be broken down into two categories:

1. Ongoing yearly fees, also called management fees.
2. Transaction fees. What you pay for when buying or selling fund shares (also called the load).

To help you understand the ongoing costs relating to each fund, the expense ratio or Managements Expense Ratio (MER) is used.

This ratio is composed of the following:

- *The fund manager's fees*. This is between 0.25% and 1.5% of assets on average.
- *Administration costs*. This is the stationary, postage, record keeping, customer service, complaints department, website management, etc.

- ***12B-1 fee*** (in the US). This is for paying brokerage commissions, advertising, and promoting the fund.

There may be other charges levied in foreign markets, so always check.

Expense ratios range from 0.2% (usually for index funds), up to 2.0% (for foreign or international funds). It is not worth paying a high expense fee for your mutual fund. There is no correlation between this fee and the performance of a fund. This is where you have to keep shopping until you get the lowest fees.

To compensate brokers and salespeople for selling the fund to new customers, the fund will pay a load to the salesperson. The cost of this load is normally transferred to you, therefore, AVOID BUYING FUNDS WITH LOADS.

Loads come in two flavours:

1. Front-end loads – If you invest $5,000 into a fund with a 5% front end load, $250 will go towards the broker or salesperson, and $4750 will be invested into the fund for you.
2. Back-end loads (also called deferred sales charges) – Typically a tiered deferred charge based on your length of holding a fund. An example is a 5% backend loaded fund that decreases to 0% in the 6th year. That means that if you sell the fund within the 1st year, you would incur a 5% charge. If you sell within the 2nd year, you would incur a 4% charge. If you sell within the 3rd year, you would incur a 3% charge. If you sell within the 4th year, you would incur a 2% charge. In addition, if you sell within the 5th year, you would incur a 1% charge.

There are no-load funds, which sell shares without commission or sales charges. Try the following sources for no-load funds:

- Schwab's OneSource (*http://www.schwab.com*)
- Vanguard's FundAccess (*http://www.vanguard.com*)
- Fidelity's   FundsNetwork (*http://personal.fidelity.com*)
- American Express (*www.americanexpress.com*)
- Ameritrade (*www.ameritrade.com*)
- Brown & Co. (*www.brownco.com*)
- Harrisdirect (*www.harrisdirect.com*)
- E*Trade (*www.etrade.com*)
- Muriel Siebert (*www.siebertnet.com*)
- Quick & Reilly (*www.quickandreilly.com*)
- Scottrade (*www.scottrade.com*)
- TDWtrhouse (*www.tdwaterhouse.com*)

When you redeem your fund, the fund is obliged by US law to send you your funds within five business days. This may be different elsewhere. See the following websites for more information:

- *http://www.mfea.com/FundSelector*
- *http://www.MorningStar.com*
- *http://screen.yahoo.com/funds.html*
- *http://moneycentral.msn.com/investor/finder/customf unds.asp*

Finding no-load funds

Field Name	Operator	Value
Front Load	=	0
Deferred Sales Charge	=	0
12b-1 Fee	=	0
Redemption Fee	=	0
Expense Ratio	<=	0
Closed to New Investors	=	False
Morningstar Rating	>=	4-star
Morningstar Risk	<=	Below Average
Morningstar Return	>=	Above Average

Figure 1: The MSN Money fund screener

For a fund screener that is quick and easy to use, try the MSN Money Fund Screener. See Figure 1 for the selection criteria for no-load funds: with a high MorningStar (value) rating and a low MorningStar Risk rating.

Because there are no charges with these, you can trade them almost like stock. You will note that the vast majority of the qualifying funds from the screener in Figure 1 are large cap, blended funds, paying dividends annually.

You have seen that there are funds for literally every investing style. If you decide to invest in a mutual fund, remember to minimise your costs as much as possible. By only investing into no-load funds, you will be able to buy and sell more frequently, and in a sense trade the fund for maximum profitability.

Do not be fooled by all the claims made by various fund prospectuses and adverts. No fund value appreciates forever. Therefore, keep moving your money where the moneymaking is good.

Chapter 3

- *Making Money with Mutual Funds*

Making Money with Mutual Funds

Most of the risks that funds attempt to reduce are only relevant to the rules and regulations relating to managing a fund. Because of this, even when a fund manager sees that their share holding is falling in a bear market he or she will not be allowed to dump all their positions. Therefore, if you are a fund member, and you did not liquidate your holdings in that fund, you too would experience these loses.

As an investor in a fund, you can liquidate your holdings at any time. If you bought the fund with no charges and there are no redemption costs, you are free to liquidate as and when you choose. Let us look at how to find no-load, no fee, and no redemption charge funds.

The process for doing this is simple. First, use your computer to visit *http://moneycentral.msn.com/investor/finder /customfunds.asp*. Once you are in the fund screener, add the criteria for Operator and Values illustrated in Figure 1. When completed, click the Run Search button.

A handful of funds that qualify will be displayed. You will notice that these funds are almost all fund of funds; therefore investing in them will provide you with a great means for diversification, low costs, high dividends, and low risk all rolled into one.

Now that you have your selection of funds to consider, you need to know the point of entry, and the length of time to stay in them. The profiles of the funds that fit this screener are all similar. They behave the same way during bull and bear markets; therefore, you can apply some simple rules to them.

To do this, first you need to determine the state of the leading world economy, namely the US markets. The NASDAQ, DOW, and S&P will give you clues as to which phase of the economic cycle the general markets are in. See Figures 2, Figure 3, and Figure 4, which illustrate this.

Making Money with Funds

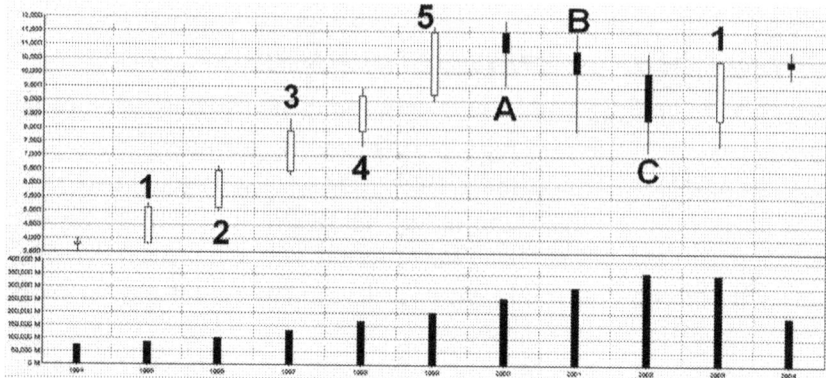

Figure 2: Long-term view of the Dow Jones Industrial Average

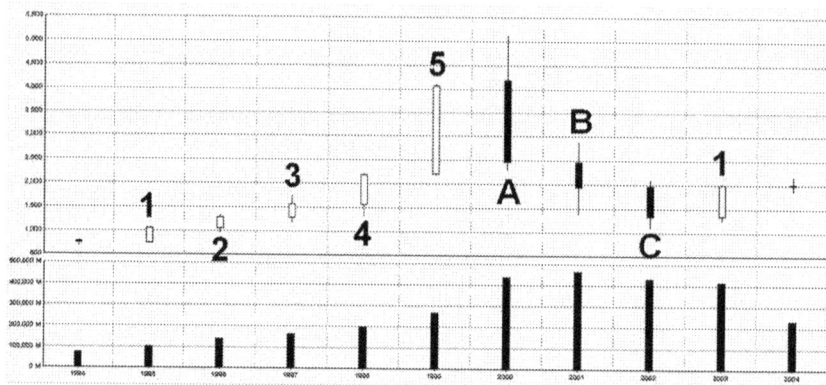

Figure 3: Long-term view of the NASDAQ Composite Index

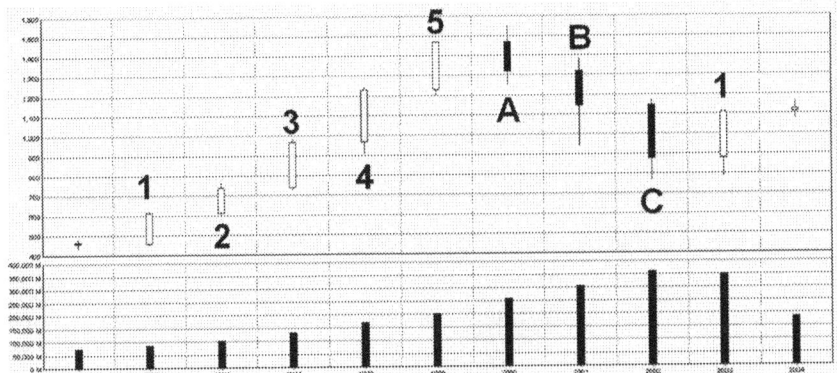

Figure 4: Long-term view of the S&P 500 Index, with yearly candlesticks

By using a long-term Elliot Wave analysis on the major markets, and by using a 10 to 15 year view with annual candlesticks, you can see that since 1995, the markets became bullish and grew in bullishness until Jan 2000, where a bear market ensued. This bear market ended in 2003.

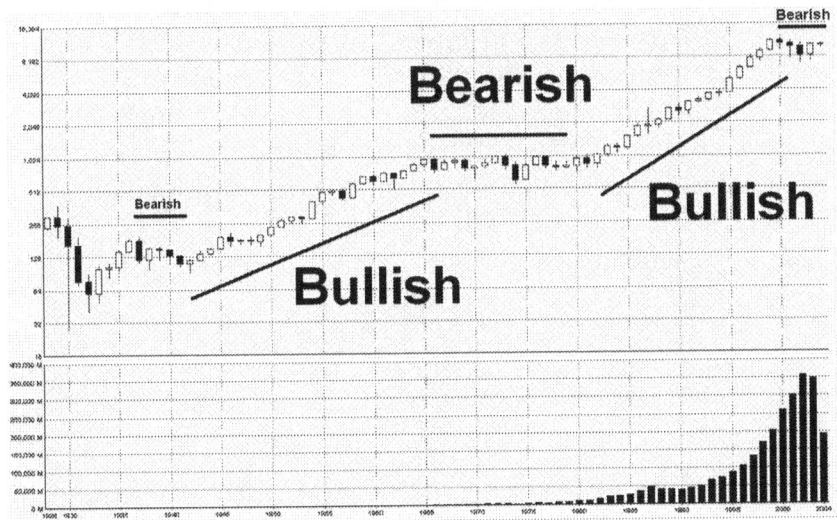

Figure 5: Dow economic cycles

From 2010 until probably 2030, we will experience another bull market. I am estimating this from the bear market of 1966 until 1978. This lasted roughly 10 years. The two bull markets you see in Figure 5 lasted roughly 20 years each. To think we are out of the bear market now would be presumptuous. I think we are experiencing a short-term bear trend now, in 2004, but the long-term bearishness will hound the markets for another 4 to 6 years. Then the markets will start out on another long-term bullish climb for another 20 years roughly.

With this in mind, you will do best to either avoid investing in these funds until another 5 years time when a long-term bearish trend initiates, or invest in them now but be prepared to review them regularly (quarterly).

How to Determine Short Term Trend

How do you review a fund to determine if you should sell or buy more? You can do this by using the Elliott Wave analysis for signalling. (Candlesticks are not available for these funds. They trade in securities that may be spread over the globe, thus the markets have overlapping opening and closing times).

I use the simplest method, moving averages. The 200-day moving average is your greatest indicator in this case. It is perfect for using to indicate when to buy or sell funds. When used in conjunction with the price movement of a fund, the 200-day MA clearly indicates crossover points in price movement. These crossover points are ideal entry and exit price indicators. The screener in Figure 1 will harvest funds that are best traded using this technique.

The 200 Day MA Fund Trading Technique

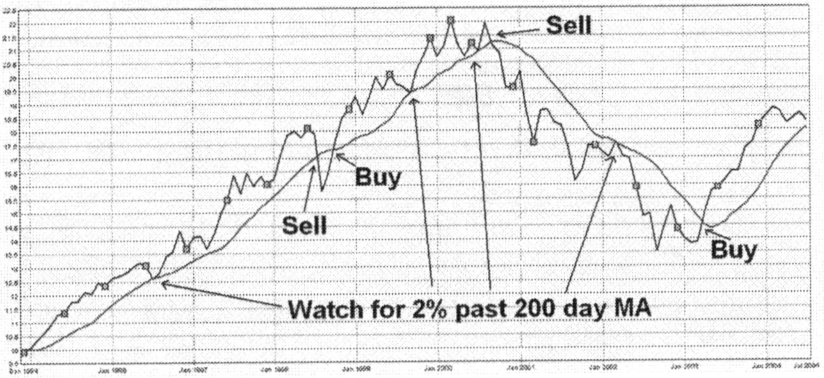

Figure 6: Using 200-day MA to signal exits and entries

Figure 6, shows the 200-day MA against a fund's 10-year chart. You should buy when the 200-day MA crosses the fund price by 2% from the point of crossing (i.e. the 200 day-MA is less than the fund price), and sell when the 200-day MA crosses the fund price by 2% from the point of crossing (i.e. the 200-day MA is greater than the fund price).

You can invest in other securities, or just wait during the times when the 200-day MA sits above the fund price (when you should be out of the fund). DO NOT USE THIS TECHNIQUE FOR ETF TRADING. This technique works best with the funds harvested from the screener in Figure 1. This is because these funds are very large with many underlying securities. This makes them move sluggishly, thus signalling the 200-day MA more reliably. By using a fund with a smaller securities base, and therefore, one that reacts too easily to market forces, you will be selling and buying too frequently, and loosing money through commissions, and through inability to profit from shorter bullish and bearish trends, (because the price will cross the 200-day MA too frequently).

You can use an alerting service to alert you when the funds you are interested in cross the 200-day MA. Your online broker should offer such an alert (see Appendix 1 for a list of online brokers). You can also use MSN Money's, or Yahoo! Finance's alerting services. You can also find fund alerting services from https://secure.globeadvisor.com, *http://www. MorningStar.com* or by searching for fund alerts on the internet.

Summary of the 200-day MA fund trading strategy

You have seen that there are two types of fund, with open-ended being the most popular fund type. Amongst the plethora of funds available, you want the few that will offer you secure and high returns, global diversification, with low or no loading (no charges or fees). With this in mind, use the screener illustrated in Figure 1. The funds that are harvested from these screeners meet our criteria of diversification, high returns, and no charges. You have also learned how to maximise your returns with these funds by trading them using the 200-day MA. With this strategy, you can be sure to be in the fund during the good times and out of the fund during the bad times.

How to Benefit From Bear Markets

The 200-day MA fund trading strategy is great however, during a bear market; you will not find many buying signals. Whilst this is great because at least you will not participate in the majority of investments making losses, it is a shame to leave your fund allocation capital not invested.

Because of this reason, I have developed a technique to milk profits from a bear market, whilst you wait for the next bull market.

ETFs come to our rescue during bear markets. Because they are traded just like shares, (i.e. they are optionable and you can sell them short), you can use them just as you would shares, namely sell them short.

How do you know when it is a bear market?

There are several ways to tell when the bear market begins. Firstly, all indexes except the Dow will cross the 200-day MA, and stay under it for over three to six months. The Dow will cross the 200-day MA but will tend to stay on, or under it, for the same periods. To see this graphically, view a 5 to 10-year chart of the major indexes with monthly candlesticks. Figure 7 has been used as an example.

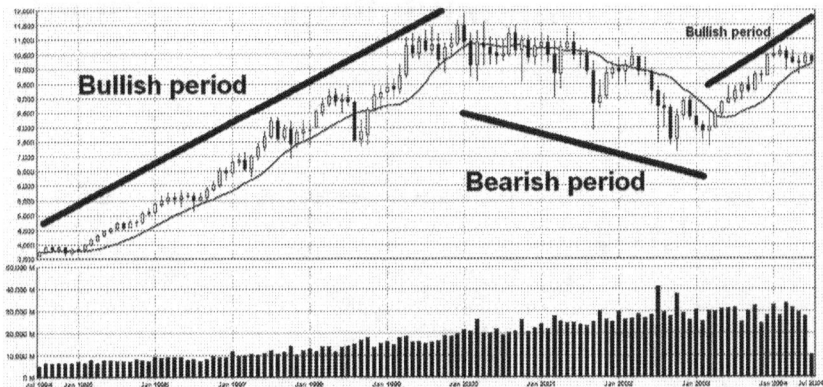

Figure 7: Dow Jones Industrial Average 10-year chart with monthly candlesticks

You will notice in Figure 7, that the majority of the candlesticks are either on the 200-day MA, or below the 200-day MA, during the bearish period. However, during the bullish periods, the majority of the candlesticks are above the 200-day MA, or on the 200-day MA.

See Appendix 2 for a list of ETFs. Let us take a quick look at the S&P, NASDAQ, and Dow.

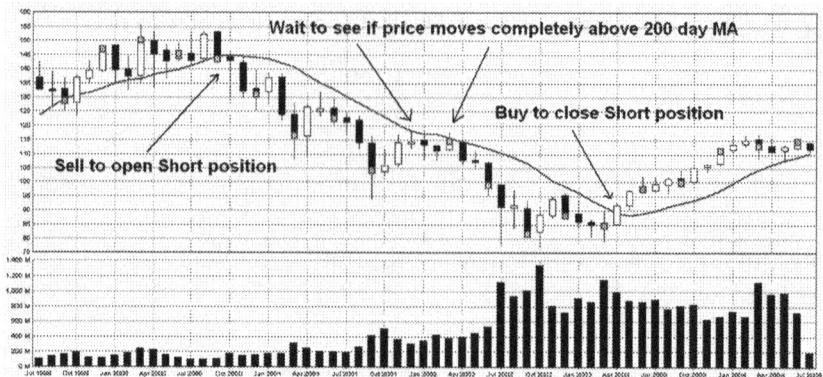

Figure 8: The S&P 100 (SPY) over 5 years

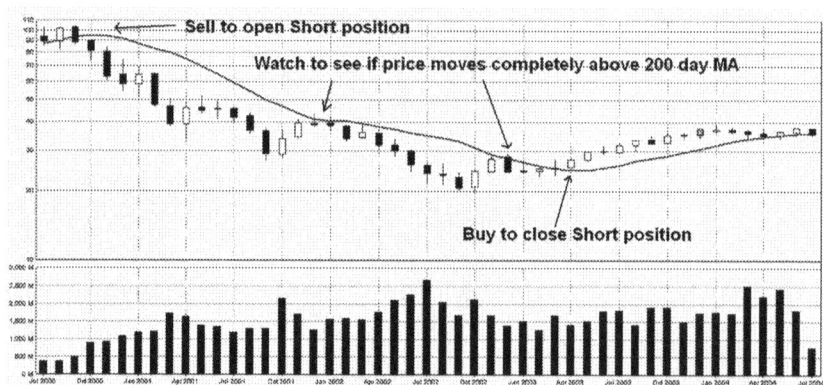

Figure 9: The NASDAQ (QQQQ) over 4 years

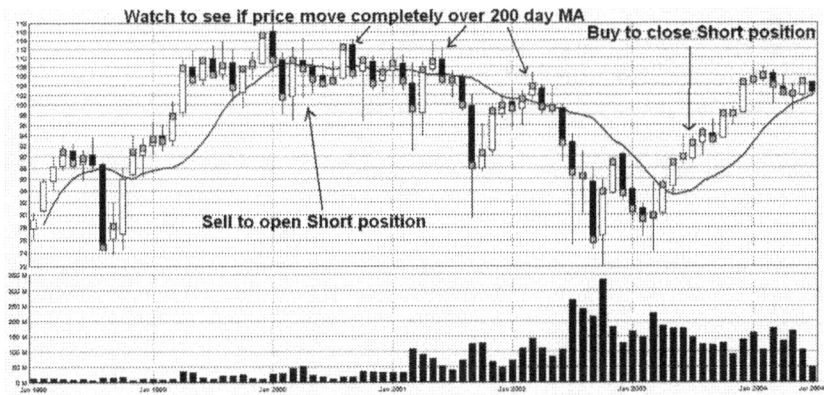

Figure 10: The Dow (DIA) over 6 years

In Figure 8, Figure 9, and Figure 10, you will see the major US ETFs. You should short them when you see their price sitting on, or underneath the 200-day MA for three-six months in a row. I say three-six months in a row, because if you are experienced at watching the market, you will know after the third month whether the index will continue down or not. However, if you are inexperienced, then go for the six-month rule. Once you have a short position in the ETF, watch out for the price to move above the 200-day MA for two to three months consecutively (i.e. when you see three white candlesticks).

As you can see from Figure 8, Figure 9, and Figure 10, the DIA is the most difficult to use this technique with. This is because when it falls, it stays near the 200-day MA. Avoid the DIA if you do not feel confident with this. The QQQQ and SPY are normally more profitable for shorting, and it is definitely easier to read their signals.

There are many ETFs, as you can see in Appendix 2. This system will work for any of them. Note that the ETFs not related to the Dow, would have the easiest signals to read.

So now, you have a system to make money with funds in the bad times and the good times. By playing both sides of the economy, you will make large double-digit percentage profits, and succeed at trading funds in any market.

Chapter 4

- *Asset Allocation*

Asset Allocation

Applying asset allocation principles to your investment portfolio will not only decrease the effects of disasters, but will help you take advantage of the inherent opportunities hidden within disasters. For instance, during a market crash, if you applied asset allocation to your investments, you would have the vast majority of your investments in secure assets that would be untouched by the market crash. Therefore, when others are wiped out, and equity and property prices are at an all time low, you can use some of your secure investments to snap up these bargains, thus reaping great profits when the market later recovers.

This is the purpose and benefit of a good asset allocated portfolio. If you do not begin with this, you could end up as I did in 2000, starting from scratch because an unexpected disaster like the March 2000 stock market crash befell me. Take heed to this wise advice. Start by allocating assets to the four categories: security, buy and hold, momentum, and lifestyle.

The only category I will not cover is Lifestyle, as it requires no help from me for you to spend your money. Notice that I left this category until last. This should be the last category to put your money in, as financially, it is a hole in the ground. Cars, designer clothes, holidays, electronic gadgets etc, will not return any interest. In some cases as with cars and private jets, they will actually cost you money to keep them. In addition to this, aim to use returns from investments to increase your lifestyle, not your salary or main income.

The proper allocation of investment funds to assets can be achieved by taking your age and current financial position into consideration. So let us get started and learn what each investment category is, and how much to allocate to it.

The three investment categories that we will now cover will be as follows:

- Security
- Buy and hold

- Momentum

Security

Security products protect you against a negative downside.[1] Examples of these are a will, life insurance, critical illness insurance, health plan, pension plan, and tax-exempt savings instruments.

Buy and Hold

These are assets both with or without tax-exemption, and with potential for a negative downside. These products do not qualify for the security category. Examples of them are shares, fine wine, diamonds, funds, and bonds, etc. These products generally have a maximum loss potential of your investment in them, as you can only loose what you put in them at the worst case.

Momentum

Momentum consists of assets with a high risk factor, offering potentially high positive upside returns, as well as potentially high negative downside losses i.e. options, futures, and spread betting etc. These products may have an unlimited loss potential as you could loose more than you originally invested in them.

Applying Asset Allocation

You should aim to invest most of your assets and investment income into security products and investments that are free from a negative downside. In addition to that, all

---

[1] Financial instruments grow in value or decrease in value. When they have the potential to grow in value, we say that they have a positive upside. When they have the potential to decrease in value, we say that have a negative downside.

investments in the security category should also be exempt from tax. We will now look at the two key considerations for determining how you apply asset allocation. These two factors are age and current financial state.

Age

Below 30

If you are at below 30 (the furthest group away from retirement age), you may want to increase your buy and hold and momentum allocations to lean more on the riskier side, as you have the time to recover from potential disasters to your buy and hold and momentum assets.

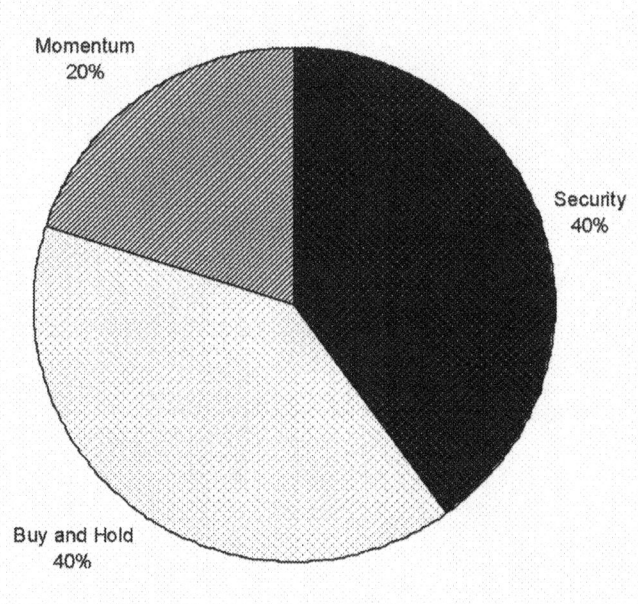

Figure 11: Furthest from retirement age - asset allocation (below 30)

30 to 50

Those in the middle-aged group of 30 to 50 should consider a more middle ground asset allocation style. Neither too risky nor too security focused.

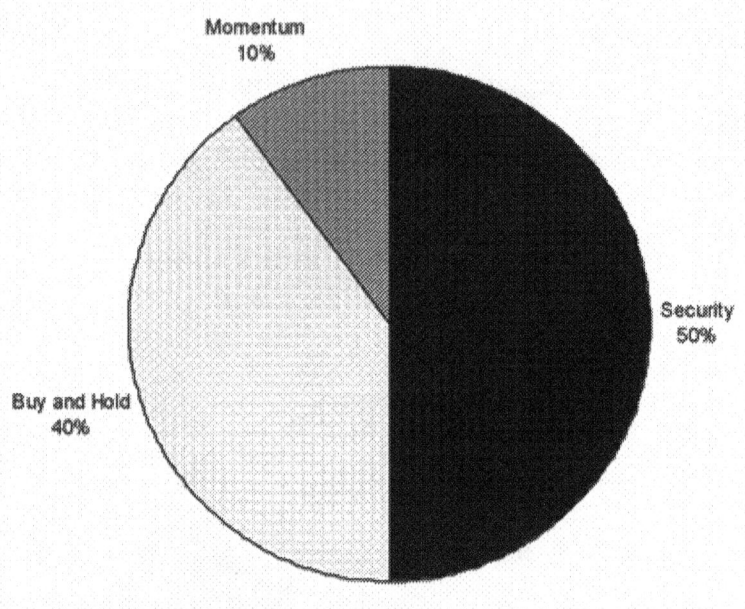

Figure 12: Middle-aged - asset allocation (30 to 50)

50 plus

Those of you who are 50 plus, and therefore close to retirement age, should increase your security allocations and decrease your riskier assets.

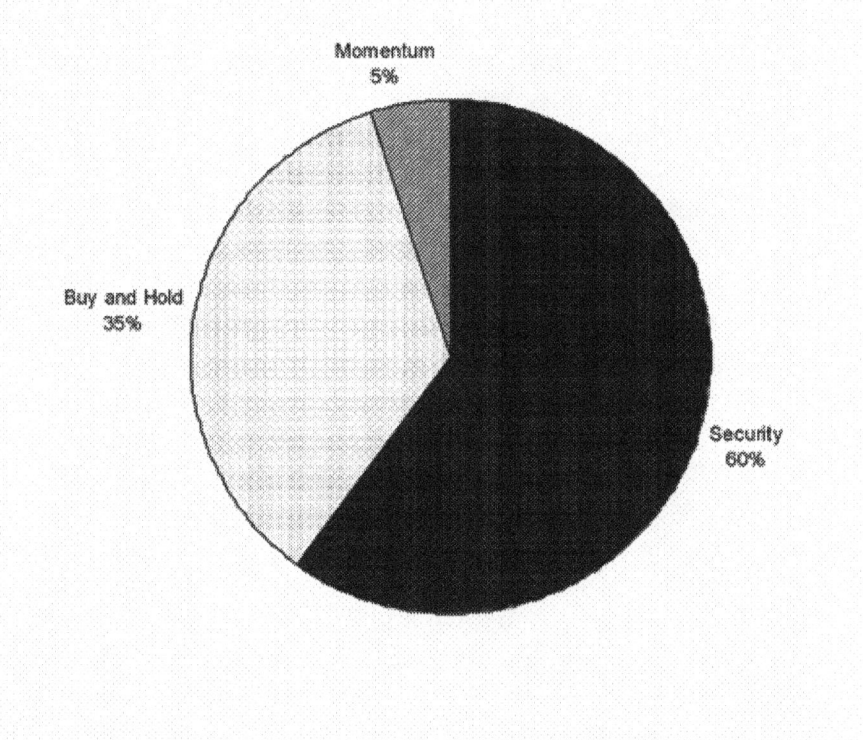

Figure 13: Near retirement age - asset allocation (50 plus)

I mentioned earlier that there were two considerations. You have looked at the first one, age. Now let us look at the second, your current financial state.

Current Financial State

We will break this section into three groups: the poor, the wealth off, and the rich.

The poor

These people should not invest in anything but security products and investments, as they cannot afford any downside risk. It does not matter how much money you earn, if you spend more than you are making then you should only invest into security products and investments (if you have any disposable income available).

Note: If you are in this category, you can get out of it by reading and applying the advice in the prequel to this book, *How to Destroy Your Debts*. Until you are no longer in this category, you should not invest in any buy and hold or momentum products, or investments.

The well off

The second group, the well off, are those who spend less than they make and have no debt, except perhaps a mortgage. If you are in this group, you will have disposable income and thus can afford to invest into buy and hold investments. For this group of readers I would advise you to apply the asset allocation illustrated in Figure 11. Until you are free from all debt, which includes your mortgage, you should not invest into any momentum products or investments.

Note: Incidentally, reading and applying *How to Destroy Your Debts* would also help those in this category, especially in clearing your mortgage in a fraction of the normal time it would otherwise take.

The rich

Those who have no debt and spend less than they make, will be able to use the age considerations covered previously, to decide how to allocate their assets.

Therefore, you can afford a little risk if you have no debts and are living within your means. A maximum of 20% of your assets (although 5%-10% is recommended), and investment income can be allocated to momentum[2]. Make sure however, that you do not lower your security allocation below 40%, no matter what your situation.

Other Considerations

If you are contemplating placing yourself in the wrong category, i.e. the Rich category, when you currently belong in another category, i.e. the poor category, you will only be delaying the time it takes to become totally financially free. You could also be worsening your situation and inviting disaster to befall you.

Do not invest more into momentum, thinking you will catch up with your security assets when you have made a fortune. You will only worsen matters, or worse still, you could end up bankrupt. If you do not want to apply the advice in this section on Asset Allocation, please do not read any further, as you can only do yourself harm.

Learn from the Egyptian pyramids. They have lasted over thousands of years because they were made to last the test of time. Make sure that your foundation for total financial freedom is made up of security products and investments. Figure 14 below illustrates the ideal secure and sturdy structure formed when this balance is implemented through correct asset allocation. As you can see, the pyramid is secure resting on a base of security. Once this secure base is established, you can

---

[2] Figure 85, Figure 86 and Figure 87 are based on the maximum allocations.

build the next level on top, buy and hold. Finally, you complete your asset allocation with a small allocation into momentum products.

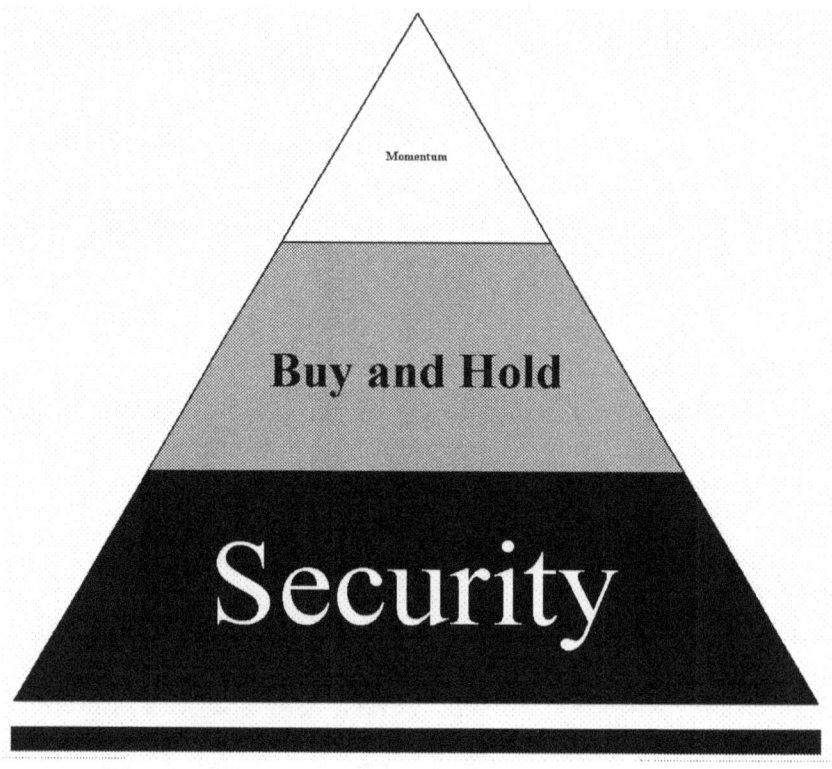

Figure 14: Ideal balanced asset allocation (N.B. momentum is represented by the white triangle above buy and hold)

In Figure 15, you can see that you will have a weak base if you invest more in buy and hold, and less in security. This structure will not stand for long. It would only take a stock market crash, or economic downturn, and your whole investment structure would topple.

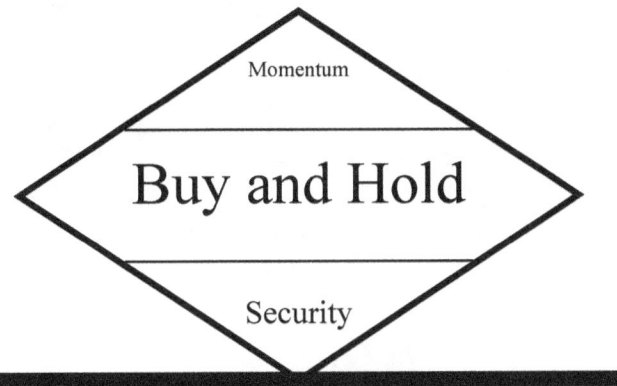

Figure 15: Over-investment in buy and hold

Looking at Figure 16 below, you will see the most volatile and dangerous structure you could build. By having most of your investments in momentum products, with few of your assets in security, you stand a chance of being completely wiped out by the slightest unexpected turn in the markets.

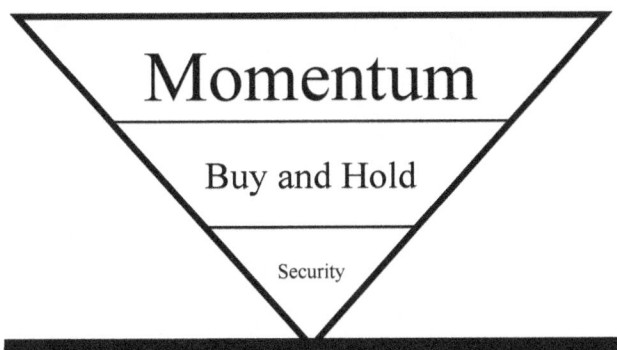

Figure 16: Over-investment into momentum

Summary to Asset Allocation

You have learned about the importance of allocating your assets and investment income according to your age and financial situation. To be successful in investing, and to build a financially secure portfolio, you will need to read and reread this section, then apply the advice.

I used to made a lot of money, and then lose it all again, and again. This cycle only stopped when I started to apply the Asset Allocation principle to my investments. To secure and guarantee your financial success, apply Asset Allocation to your assets and investments. Then when a disaster comes along, you will be better protected.

Come back to this section whenever you go off course. Asset Allocation is the most important subject I will cover for achieving financial success through investments.

Chapter 5

- ***Placing Your Trades***

Placing Your Trades

Before you begin trading with real money, you need to understand how to place a trade.

You can place your trade with a broker via phone, fax, email, or on the internet. Most Brokerage firms only take orders via the internet or phone. The cheapest method is normally via the internet. You will need to know the symbol for the fund you want to buy. There are several options you have when placing your trade. These are as follows:

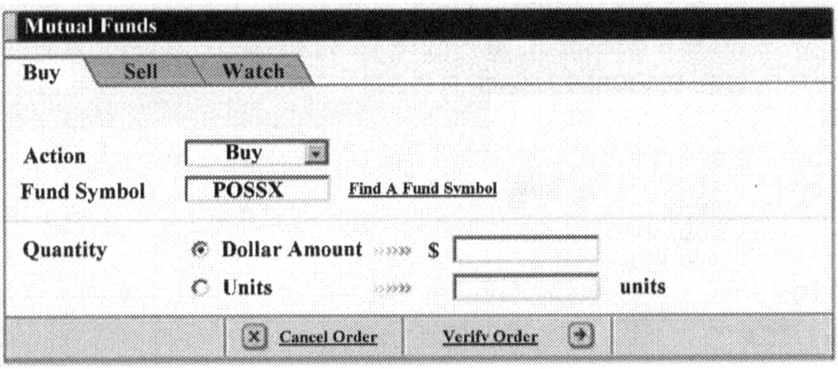

Figure 17: Example of an order form

Action – this is where you specify whether you want to buy (long) funds or sell (short) ETFs. If you already own the fund, you can specify to Sell. If you have sold short and want to Buy to Cover, you can also do this.

Symbol – type the funds symbol here (i.e. POSSX etc). If you do not know the symbol but know the Fund name, your broker's order page will have a find symbol button to allow you to find the fund symbol.

Quantity – In this section of the order form, you specify how many units of the fund you want to buy. If you were spending your total balance, this would be:

(Your account balance – commission charges) /price of fund = Number of units you can afford.

If you are using margin as well as your account balance, add the margin value to your account balance, and use this as your account balance in the equation above.

Note in Figure 17, that you can buy using the dollar amount or the units. Most brokers offer this option.

If you are trading ETFs you will likely be using a stock trade order sheet. In Figure 18 an example is offered with explanations for each section.

Buy / Sell Your Stock

Action: ⊙ Buy   Number of shares: Symbol:
         ○ Sell
         ○ Buy to cover   **Find Symbol**
         ○ Sell short

Term: | Limit ▾ | Price:

Good for: | Day   ▾ | Special Instructions: | No Special Instructions ▾ |
          | .. ▾ | .. ▾ | .. ▾ |

Preview Order

Figure 18: Example of an order form

Action – this is where you specify whether you want to buy (long) shares or sell (short) shares. If you already own the stock, you can specify to Sell. If you have sold short and want to Buy to Cover, you can also do this.

Number of Shares – In this section of the order form, you specify how many shares of the stock you want to buy. If you were spending your total balance, this would be:

50

(Your account balance – commission charges) /price of stock = Number of shares you can afford.

If you are using margin as well as your account balance, add the margin value to your account balance, and use this as your account balance in the equation above.

Symbol – type the stocks symbol here (i.e. QQQQ etc). If you do not know the symbol but know the company name, your broker's order page will have a find symbol button to allow you to find the companies symbol.

Term – This may also be called order type. This is where you select from one of the following:

- *Market*. Select this type of order if you want to purchase at the current market price. You have to select good for day, in the Good for section
- *Limit* Select this type of order if you want to buy at a specified price when the share price reaches a fixed price. You have to specify this price. This specified price has to be greater than the current price if a long order, and less than the current price if a short order.
- *Stop Market* Select this type of order if you want to place a market order when the price gets to a set price.
- *Stop Limit* Select this type of order if you want to place a limit order when the price gets to a set price.
- *Trailing Stop* Select this type of order if you want to place a stop limit at a set point, or a percentage behind the current price. Keep moving this stop limit as the stock moves in price. Not all brokers may offer this option.

Price – if you selected any term except Market, you will need to specify a price.

Good for – this is where you specify how long you want the order to stay active. You can select one of the following:

- *Day* – Your order will stay open until end of the trading day. Normally, market orders are filled within seconds of placing them. (This option must be selected when placing a market order).
- *Market on close (MOC)* – This is a buy or sell order which is to be executed as a market order as close as possible to the end of the day.
- *End of week (EOW)* – This order lasts until end of trading on Friday.
- *End of month (EOM)* – This order stays open until end of day, on the last trading day of the month.
- *Good until cancelled (GTC)* – This order stays open for 90 days.
- *Good through date (GTD)* – This order stays open through the date you specify.

Special instructions – This is where you specify any other instructions you want associated with the order. You will normally be presented with the following list:

- No special instruction.
- All or none (AON) – Fill all your order or none of it.
- Do not reduce (DNR) – Do not fill in smaller batches.
- Fill or kill (FOK) – Fill the order or cancel the order.

- AON/DNR – Fill all or none/do not fill in smaller bathes.

Once you have specified all the order criteria, you can preview your order and confirm it if the preview is correct. Market orders are the cheapest order type. I never use market orders because I find the market makers always sell market orders at a premium. The only time this is not true is when buying large caps or blue chips. These companies have such huge volumes that the market makers can afford to have smaller margins.

Main points to remember
Never use market orders, always use a limit order, and specify the price you wish to purchase. Never be in a hurry to own a fund. You make mistakes when you are desperate. During the day, the fund price will fluctuate to its daily highs and its daily lows. Always aim to buy at discount. Set the price to what you calculated through your Fibonacci or other indicator, and place a limit order to catch the stock at that price. In a very short period, you will discover that you actually made a handsome profit by not using market orders. As your profits and investments grow, the commission for your trades will shrink in comparison with your investments size.

Practicing

Before you go live and start using real money, apply to one of the virtual portfolios offered by your broker, MSN Money, or Yahoo! Finance. You can build a portfolio there by trading real ETF's with virtual money. If you find you are making double digit profits in ten successive trades, then you may be ready to use your hard-earned cash to trade.

For information on trading games and virtual portfolios, see the following websites:

1. Bloomberg.com
   http://www.bloomberg.com/mag/pjump.html?sidenav=front

2. Briefing.com
   http://fast.quote.com/fq/briefing/fqportfolio?mode=quote&page=port

3. Zacks.com
   http://my.zacks.com/index.php3

4. MSN Money
   http://moneycentral.msn.com/investor/controls/setup.asp?Symbol=&target=/investor/charts/charting.asp

5. Forbes.com: Tools
   http://www.forbes.com/tools

6. Barchart.com
   http://equities.barchart.com/portfolio.htx

7. ClearStation.com
   http://www.clearstation.com/cgi-bin/drill_portfolio

8. Financial Times
   http://mwportfolio.ft.com/custom/ft-com/portfolio/view.asp

9. QuoteTracker.com
   http://www.QuoteTracker.com

10. NASDAQ.com
    http://www.nasdaq.com/asp/portfoliojava.asp?

11. TheStreet.com
    http://www.thestreet.com/tsc/moneynetland.html

12. Yahoo! Finance
   http://finance.yahoo.com/?u

13. Raging Bull
   http://finance.lycos.com/home/portfolio/intro.asp

14. CBS MarketWatch
   http://cbs.marketwatch.com/portfolio/default.asp?siteid=
mktw

15. Silicon Investor
   http://www.siliconinvestor.com/customize/login.gsp?ret=
   %2Fportfolio%2Findex.gsp

16. StockHouse.com
   http://www.stockhouse.com/members/login.asp?url=../po
   rtfolio/index.asp

17. MSN Money
   http://moneycentral.msn.com/scripts/webquote.dll?iPage
=pmx

18. Briefing.com
   http://fast.quote.com/fq/briefing/fqportfolio_edit

19. Stockpoint.com
   http://www.stockpoint.com/leftnav/login.asp

20. Auditrack.com
   http://auditrack.com

Conclusion

There are many ways to invest into the equity (stocks) and debt (bonds) markets. However, a fund offers an extra level of security for doing so through the provision of a professional management team, diversification, and simplicity. All these benefits also introduce some disadvantages. These disadvantages are mainly due to the charges and management fees levied by fund managers and fund brokers.

In this book, you have learned how to avoid these disadvantages by using no-load funds and through the application of simple and easy to apply techniques, to trade your own fund portfolio. Techniques for bull as well as bear markets have been provided so that no matter the market trend, you too can make double digit profits by trading mutual funds.

Appendices

Appendix 1

Online Broker List

- **A.B. Watley** – *www.abwatley.com*. Offers NASDAQ II real-time quotes and trades, from $10.
- *Accutrade* – *www.accutrade.com*. $30 per trade up to 1000 shares. Online trading requires free proprietary software. Also offers mutual funds and options trading. Margin rate is 1-2% above the brokerage call rate. $5000 minimum account balance. One notable feature is the ability to place trades at a future time when specific conditions are met. Compatible with Sharp's Zaurus PDA.
- **AFTrader** – *www.aftrader.com*. $9.95 per trade, wireless trading at no extra charge, free news alerts, free premium research, no fee IRAs, and free unlimited real-time quotes.
- **American Express Brokerage** – *http://br1.americanexpress.com/amex/bu/ fd/cda/main/0,1484,L-2,00.asp*. $14.95 per trade for up to 3000 shares. Also offers mutual funds trading. No minimum account balance. News, quotes, alerts, company research, S&P MarketScope, and Comtex are included.
- **Ameritrade** – *http://www.ameritrade.com*. $8 per market orders, $13 per limit orders. Also options, mutual funds, and bonds.
- **Amerivest** – *http://www.amerivestinc.com*
- **Atlantic Financial** - *http://www.atlanticfinancial.com*
- **Bidwell & Co.** – *http://www.bidwell.com/*. Starting at $12 per trade.
- **Boom** – *http://www.boom.com*. Hong Kong.
- **Brown & Co**. – *http://www.brownco.com*. Cheapest. $5 per trade for market orders, $10 per trade for limit

orders. 100 real time quotes per trade. They only want investors with five years of experience.

- **Brunswick Direct** – *http://www.brunswickdirect.com*. Focused solely on 22 emerging markets.
- **Burch & Company** – *http://www.thetradersclub.com*. Fees from $9.95 to $14.95.
- **Bush Burns** – *http://www.bushburns.com*. $25 per trade.
- **Charles Schwab** – *http://www.schwab.com*. Allows you to buy and sell stocks, mutual funds, options, and treasuries. $30 trades up to 1000 shares, or 3 cents a share for more than 1000 shares. They also offer 50 real-time quotes per trade, plus research from Credit Suisse First Boston, Hambrecht, and Quist for $30 per month. $5000 minimum account balance.
- **Citibank** – http://www.citibank.com. Online banking and trading.
- **CompuTEL** – *http://www.computel.com*. $9 per trade for market orders for 1000 to 5000 shares, one cent per share additional over 5000 shares. $19 per trade for limit orders. Also options. 100 free real time quotes per day. No-fee IRAs. $5000 minimum opening balance.
- **Credit Suisse First Boston Australia Equities Private Limited** – *http://www. csfbaep.com.au*. Australia.
- **CyberCorp** – *http://www.cybercorp.com/default.asp*. Online broker that caters to active traders. Subsidiary of Schwab.
- **Datek** – *http://www.datek.com*. $10 per NASDAQ and NYSE trades. Unlimited real time quotes. 1-minute order execution or it is free. In addition, you can set price limits for your stocks and they will email you when the conditions are met. $2000 minimum account balance.

- **Delta Equity Services** – *http://www.deltaequity.com*. $35 plus half a percent of the total amount.
- **D.F. Mainland Group** – *http://www.dfmainland.co.nz*. New Zealand.
- **Discover Brokerage Direct** – *http://www.discoverbrokerage.com*. $15 per trade. Also offers mutual funds, options, and bond trading (including treasuries). Fee-based package adds research from Morgan Stanley, news, real time quotes, and portfolio management. Margin rate is 0.75 to 2.5% above the brokerage call rate. $2000 minimum account balance.
- **CSFB Direct** – *http://www.csfbdirect.com*. $20 per trade for up to 1000 shares. Also options, bonds and mutual funds. No minimum account balance. Excellent information package including S&P MarketScope, Zacks analyst recommendations, 100 real time stock and option quotes per trade, Reuters market news, and Lipper mutual fund researChâteau. Also, research from Donaldson Lufkin Jenrette. Integration with pagers and handhelds.
- **Dreyfus** – *http://www.edreyfus.com*. $15 per trade (first three trades are free). Best rate on options: $1.75 per contract with a $15 minimum. Real-time quotes when ordering. Margin rate is 0.5 to 1% above the brokerage call rate. $1000 minimum account balance, $2000 for margin accounts.
- **EquityStation.com** – *http://www.equitystation.com*. Caters to active investors. $19.95 market orders for 1-99 trades a month, $16.95 per trade for 100-299 trades a month, and $14.95 per trade for 300+ trades a month (price change is retroactive).
- **EmpireNow.com** – *http://www.lowfees.com*. $7 for market orders, $12 for limit orders. Market orders of 1000+ shares of stocks above $5 per share are commission-free. Also options, bonds and mutual funds. No minimum balance.

- **E*TRADE** – *http://www.etrade.com*. $15 per trade for up to 5000 shares on market orders of listed stocks, $20 for unlisted stocks and limit orders up to 5000 shares. Includes portfolio tracking system (with alerts), current market data, candlestick charts, and other technical analysis tools. Real-time quotes $30 per month. Also offers options and bonds. $5 to talk to a live broker. Margin rate: 1.75-2.25% over brokerage call rate. $1000 minimum account balance, $2000 for margin accounts. The site also includes a trading demo so you can see how everything works. Some access to IPOs at the offering price.
- **Fidelity** – *http://personal.fidelity.com/trade/index.html*. $29 per trade for up to 1000 shares. Unlimited real time quotes. Investment research from Salomon Smith Barney, plus access to IPOs.
- **Fifth Third Bank** – *http://www.53.com*
- **TheFinancialCafe.com** – *http://www.financialcafe.com*. Free market order electronic trades, $4.95 limit order electronic trades, online banking, mortgage, and insurance.
- **First Discount Brokerage** – *http://www.1db.com*. Offers full service, discount, and online brokerages services.
- **Firstrade** – *http://www.firstrade.com*. $10 per order, $5 per NASDAQ order over 1000 shares.
- **FreeTrade.com** – *http://www.freetrade.com*. Free equity trades, $5 stop and limit orders.
- **FREETRADEZ** – *http://www.freetradez.com*. Online broker offering 100% commission free trades (ad-based revenue).
- **Freedom Investments** – *http://www.freedominvestments.com*. $15 per trade.
- **Freeman Welwood** – *http://www.freemanwelwood.com*. $15 per trade for market orders, $20 per trade for limit orders up to

2000 shares. Above 2000 shares are one cent per share.

- **GE Financial Brokerage** – *http://www.gefn.com/gebrokerage/index .html*
- **Global Access** – *http://www.globefin.net*. NASDAQ Level II trading as low as $9.95 for unlimited shares.
- **Harris InvestorLine** – *http://www.harrisinvestorline.com*. $13 per trade for market orders, $18 per trade for limit orders.
- **Hoyou Barnes NetInvestor** – *http://www.netinvestor.com*. Commissions are $19 + $0.01 per share. In addition, mutual funds, bonds, options, and CDs. Portfolio tracking, news, and researChâteau $5000 minimum account balance.
- **Interactive Broker** – *http://www.interactivebrokers.com*
- **INTLTRADER.com** – *http://www.intltrader.com*. Trades in foreign and domestic securities.
- **Investex Securities Group** – *http://www.investexpress.com*. $15 per trade for most trades. Also mutual funds, options, and bonds. No minimum account balance.
- **InvestIN** – *http://www.investin.com*. $10 per trade. Free real-time quotes.
- **InvestorLine** – *http://www.investorline.com*. $25 per trade for market orders. From the Bank of Montreal. Also mutual funds.
- **InvesTrade** – *http://www.investrade.com*. $8 per trade for stocks. Automated touch-tone phone trading at the same price. An options trade is charged at $1.75 per contract, $15 minimum.
- **Jack White & Co** – *http://www.jackwhiteco.com*. Commissions start at $12 per trade. Free real-time quotes with an account. Also offers mutual funds. $5000 minimum account balance.
- **J.B. Oxford** – *http://www.jboxford.com*. Commissions start at $14.50 per trade. Unlimited real

time quotes. Also offers mutual funds, bonds, and options trading. $2000 minimum account balance. Customers receive free internet access as long as they keep the minimum balance in the account.

- **Killiney Investments** – *http://www.fin-trade.com*. A brokerage company which offers internet based dealing service in FX, futures, options, and stocks for both institutional and private investors.
- **InternetTrading** – *http://www.internettrading.com*
- **LiveTrade.com** – *http://www.livetrade.com*. Live Level 2 screens, execution via all ECNs, NYSE, and portfolio management.
- **LowTrades.com** – *http://www.lowtrades.com*. This online broker offers limit orders and market orders for $4 per trade. Do your research with InvestorGuide Research (*http://investorguide.com/researChâteauhtm*) and place cheap orders here.
- **Market Touch Web** – *http://www.bsdmtweb.com*. $15 per trade under 1000 shares.
- **MB Trading** – *http://www.mbtrading.com*. Day trading. $15 to $24 per trade.
- **Muriel Siebert & Co.** – *http://www.msiebert.com*. $15 per trade.
- **Mr. Stock** – *http://www.mrstock.com*. $15 per trade up to 1000 shares. Also offers mutual funds and options.
- **Mydiscountbroker.com** – *http://www.mydiscountbroker.com*. $12 per trade up to 5000 shares.
- **National Discount Brokers** – *http://www.ndb.com*. $14.75 per trade for market orders, $19.75 per trade for limit orders. Real time quotes. Over 7500 mutual funds. $2000 minimum account balance.
- **Net-Invest** – *http://www.net-invest.com*. From Capital International Securities Group. $25 per trade. Also in Spanish.

- **NetVest** – *http://www.netvest.com.* Discount Broker.
- **NobleTrading** – *http://www.nobletrading.com.* Online direct access brokerage firm offering choice of per share and per trade commission schedules. Trade using RealTick, E-Signal with order entry, The Shield, and the NobleTrader Level 2. Commission schedule ranges from $9.95 to $14.95, or 1.5 cents to one cent per share.
- **Norwest** – *http://www.norwest.com.*
- **Peremel Online** – *http://www.peremel.com.*
- **Quick and Reilly** – *http://www.quick-reilly.com.* $15 per trade for market orders, or $20 for limit orders. Also offers options trading. No minimum account balance. Two ways to trade, including one with the aid of a broker.
- **Regal** – *http://www.eregal.com.* $20 for NASDAQ trades of 1000 or more shares, $25 below 1000 shares, and $29 for listed trades up to 5000 shares. Unlimited real time quotes. No minimum account balance. Every tenth trade is free. Margin rate is 0.5% above the brokerage call rate.
- **R. J. Thompson Securities** – *http://www.rjt.com/default.html*
- **RML Trading** – *http://www.rmltrading.com.*
- **RushTrade.com** – *http://www.rushtrade.com.*
- **Sanford Securities** – *http://www.sanford.com.au.* Australia.
- **Schwab** – *http://www.schwab.com.* Allows you to buy and sell stocks, mutual funds, options, and treasuries. $30 trades up to 1000 shares, or 3 cents a share for more than 1000 shares. They also offer 50 real-time quotes per trade, plus research from Credit Suisse First Boston and Hambrecht and Quist for $30 per month. $5000 minimum account balance.
- **ScoTTrade** – *http://www.scottrade.com.* $7 per trade for market orders, $12 per trade for limit orders. 100

real time quotes per trade. $2,000 account minimum.
Also options trading.

- **ShareBuilder** – *http://www.sharebuilder.com*. Buy
and sell stocks in dollar amounts. No account or
investment minimums. Only $2 per transaction.
- **Sharex.com** – *http://www.sharex.com*.
- **Sherry Bruce's State Discount Brokers** –
http://www.state-discount.com.
- **Sloan Securities** – *http://www.sloansecurities.com*.
- **SuccessTrade.com** – *http://www.successtrade.com*.
For daytraders - $7.95 per trade for market and limit
orders.
- **Summit Trading** – *http://www.summittrading.com*.
Day trading. Downloadable software.
- **SpeedTrader** – *http://www.speedtrader.com*. $15 to
$20 per trade.
- **Stockwalk.com** – *http://www.stockwalk.com*. Trade
bonds and CDs, too.
- **SuccessTrade** – *http://www.successtrade.com*. All
Trades only $9.95 a trade-includes market and limit
orders.
- **Sunlogic** – *http://www.sunlogic.com*. $16 per trade.
- **Tradefast** – *https://www.tradeoptions.com*. 3 cents
per share, $20 minimum.
- **Trade4Less** – *http://www.trade4less.com*.
- **TradeScape.com** – *http://www.tradescape.com*.
Geared toward active traders. $1.50 per 100 shares,
free Level II quotes, Direct ECN connections.
Educational products.
- **TradeSecurities.com** –
http://www.tradesecurities.com. After-hours trading.
$25,000 minimum account balance. Commissions of
6 cents per share, minimum $100.
- **TradeWallStreet.com** –
http://www.tradewallstreet.com. Full service broker
providing direct access trading from $9.95 per trade.

- **TradeWell** – *http://www.trade-well.com*.
- **Trading Direct** – *http://www.tradingdirect.com*. From York Securities. Commissions start at $10 per trade. Also offers options and mutual funds. No minimum account balance.
- **Trend Trader** – *http://www.trendtrader.com*. Day trading. Starts at $15 per trade.
- **T. Royou Price** – *http://www.troweprice.com/brokerage/index.html*. $25 per trade up to 1000 shares.
- **TruTrade** – *http://www.trutrade.com*. $11 per trade for OTC or less than 2000 shares of listed stocks. No-fee IRA, free checkwriting, mutual funds, and low margin rates.
- **USRica.com** – *http://www.usrica.com*. Trades executed for only $4.95 per trade, plus $2.50 service charge. Free unlimited real-time quotes, online account balance.
- **Vision Trade** – *http://www.visiontrade.com*. $15 per stock trade. Also offers options and mutual funds.
- **Wachovia** – *http://www.wachovia.com*.
- **WR Hambrecht** – *http://www.wrhambrecht.com*. Online broker offering $20 internet and $25 broker-assisted trades
- **Wall Street Access** – *http://www.wsaccess.com*. They focus on the active trader. Commissions start at $25 per trade. 100 free real-time quotes with each trade. Also offers Treasuries and options trading.
- **Wall Street Discount** – *http://www.wsdc.com*. Starts at $20 per trade.
- **Wall Street Electronica** – *http://www.wallstreete.com*. From Winston Rodgers & Otalvaro, a full-service firm. Commissions start at $15 per trade. Also offers bonds and options. $10,000 minimum account balance.
- **Wang** – *http://www.wangvest.com*. Commissions start at $5 per trade. Text is in Chinese or English.

- **Waterhouse webBroker** –
  http://www.waterhouse.com. $12 per trade up to 5,000 shares. Free real-time quotes, charts, news, S&P reports, and Zacks earnings estimates. Also offers mutual funds. 24-hour access to a live broker.
- **Web Street Securities** –
  http://www.webstreetsecurities.com. $15 per trade. NASDAQ trades of 1000 or more shares are commission-free. Ten second executions and one minute email confirmations. Streaming real-time portfolio management. Java-based interface.
- **WellsTrade** – *http://wellsfargo.com/wellstrade*. From Wells Fargo. $30 per trade.
- **White Discount Securities Online** – *http://www.wdsonline.com*.
- **Wit Capital** – *http://www.witcapital.com*. Stocks, mutual funds, and options.
- **Wyse** – *http://www.wyse-sec.com*. Starts at $8 per trade.
- **Your Discount Broker** – *http://www.ydb.com*. Day traders can pay $30 to trade in and out of any stock for a full day.

Appendix 2

Exchange Traded Funds (ETFs)

Name	*Category*	*StyleBox*
NASDAQ 100 Trust Shares (QQQQ)	Large Growth	
SPDRs (SPY)	Large Blend	
Semiconductor HOLDRs (SMH)	Specialty-Technology	
iShares MSCI Japan Index (EWJ)	Japan Stock	
iShares Russell 2000 Index (IWM)	Small Blend	
DIAMONDS Trust, Series 1 (DIA)	Large Blend	
Financial Select Sector SPDR (XLF)	Specialty-Financial	
Biotech HOLDRs (BBH)	Specialty-Health	
Telecom HOLDRs (TTH)	Specialty-Communications	
Energy Select Sector SPDR (XLE)	Specialty-Natural Res	
Industrial Select Sector SPDR (XLI)	Large Value	
Utilities HOLDRs (UTH)	Specialty-Utilities	
iShares Nasdaq Biotechnology (IBB)	Specialty-Health	
Utilities Select Sector SPDR (XLU)	Specialty-Utilities	
Health Care Select Sect SPDR (XLV)	Large Blend	
MidCap SPDRs (MDY)	Mid-Cap Blend	
Consumer Staples Select Sector SPDR (XLP)	Large Blend	
iShares MSCI EAFE Index Fund (EFA)	Foreign Large Blend	
iShares Russell 1000 Value Index (IWD)	Large Value	
Regional Bank HOLDRs (RKH)	Specialty-Financial	
iShares Dow Jones US Real Estate (IYR)	Specialty-Real Estate	
Technology Select Sector SPDR (XLK)	Specialty-Technology	
iShares Lehman 20+ Year Treas Bond (TLT)	Long Government	---
iShares Russell 2000 Value Index (IWN)	Small Value	
Telebras HOLDRs (TBH)	Latin America Stock	---
iShares Russell 2000 Growth Index (IWO)	Small Growth	
iShares Dow Jones Select Dividend Index (DVY)	Mid-Cap Value	
Internet HOLDRs (HHH)	Specialty-Technology	
iShares S&P 500 Index (IVV)	Large Blend	
iShares Lehman 1-3 Year Treasury Bond	Short Government	---

Fund	Category
(SHY)	
iShares MSCI United Kingdom Index (EWU)	Europe Stock
Pharmaceutical HOLDRs (PPH)	Specialty-Health
iShares MSCI South Korea Index (EWY)	Pacific/Asia ex-Japan Stk
Powershares Dynamic Market (PWC)	Large Blend
iShares Goldman Sachs Semiconductor (IGW)	Specialty-Technology
iShares S&P SmallCap 600/BARRA Growth (IJT)	Small Growth
Materials Select Sector SPDR (XLB)	Large Blend
streetTRACKS DJ US Small Cap Growth (DSG)	Small Growth
iShares S&P 500/BARRA Value Index (IVE)	Large Value
iShares MSCI Brazil (Free) Index (EWZ)	Latin America Stock
iShares MSCI Taiwan Index (EWT)	Pacific/Asia ex-Japan Stk
iShares Goldman Sachs Networking (IGN)	Specialty-Technology
iShares S&P SmallCap 600 Index (IJR)	Small Blend
iShares MSCI Emerg Mkts Index (EEM)	Diversified Emerging Mkts
streetTRACKS DJ US Large Cap Growth (ELG)	Large Growth
iShares MSCI Austria Index (EWO)	Europe Stock
iShares MSCI Singapore (Free) Index (EWS)	Pacific/Asia ex-Japan Stk
iShares S&P SmallCap 600/BARRA Value (IJS)	Small Value
iShares Lehman 7-10 Year Treasury (IEF)	Intermediate Government
iShares MSCI Mexico (Free) Index (EWW)	Latin America Stock
iShares Russell Midcap Growth Index (IWP)	Mid-Cap Growth
iShares Goldman Sachs Technology Indx (IGM)	Specialty-Technology
iShares MSCI Hong Kong Index (EWH)	Pacific/Asia ex-Japan Stk
iShares S&P 500/BARRA Growth Index (IVW)	Large Growth
iShares Russell 1000 Growth Index (IWF)	Large Growth
iShares Russell 3000 Index (IWV)	Large Blend
iShares Russell Midcap Value Index (IWS)	Mid-Cap Value

iShares GS $ InvestTop Corp Bond (LQD)	Intermediate-Term Bond	---
Internet Infrastructure HOLDRs (IIH)	Specialty-Technology	⊞
iShares Cohen & Steers Realty Majors (ICF)	Specialty-Real Estate	⊞
iShares Russell 1000 Index (IWB)	Large Blend	⊞
iShares Russell 3000 Growth Index (IWZ)	Large Growth	⊞
B2B Internet HOLDRs (BHH)	Specialty-Technology	⊞
Consumer Discretionary SPDR (XLY)	Large Blend	⊞
iShares MSCI Australia Index (EWA)	Foreign Large Blend	⊞
iShares S&P MidCap 400 Index (IJH)	Mid-Cap Blend	⊞
iShares Lehman Aggregate Bond (AGG)	Intermediate-Term Bond	---
streetTRACKS DJ US Large Cap Value (ELV)	Large Value	⊞
iShares Goldman Sachs Software Index (IGV)	Specialty-Technology	⊞
iShares S&P MidCap 400/BARRA Value (IJJ)	Mid-Cap Value	⊞
iShares S&P 100 Index (OEF)	Large Growth	⊞
iShares Lehman TIPS Bond (TIP)	Long Government	---
Fresco Dow Jones Euro STOXX 50 (FEZ)	Europe Stock	⊞
iShares Dow Jones US Healthcare (IYH)	Specialty-Health	⊞
iShares Dow Jones US Consumer Cycl (IYC)	Large Blend	⊞
iShares S&P Global Energy Sector (IXC)	Specialty-Natural Res	⊞
Vanguard Total Stock Market VIPERs (VTI)	Large Blend	⊞
Vanguard Small Cap Growth VIPERs (VBK)	Small Growth	⊞
Fidelity Nasdaq Composite Index Tracking (ONEQ)	Large Growth	⊞
iShares Dow Jones US Cons Non-Cycl (IYK)	Large Blend	⊞
iShares MSCI Malaysia (Free) Index (EWM)	Pacific/Asia ex-Japan Stk	⊞
iShares Dow Jones US Utilities (IDU)	Specialty-Utilities	⊞
iShares MSCI Germany Index (EWG)	Europe Stock	⊞
Vanguard Small Cap Value VIPERS (VBR)	Small Value	⊞
iShares Dow Jones US Energy (IYE)	Specialty-Natural Res	⊞
iShares Russell Midcap Index (IWR)	Mid-Cap Blend	⊞

71

Fund	Category	
iShares Dow Jones US Basic Materials (IYM)	Large Value	⊞
iShares MSCI Canada Index (EWC)	Foreign Large Value	⊞
Broadband HOLDRs (BDH)	Specialty-Communications	⊞
iShares Dow Jones US Total Market Ind (IYY)	Large Blend	⊞
Rydex S&P Equal Weight (RSP)	Large Blend	⊞
iShares Dow Jones US Telecom (IYZ)	Specialty-Communications	⊞
iShares Dow Jones US Technology (IYW)	Specialty-Technology	⊞
iShares Dow Jones Transportation Average (IYT)	Mid-Cap Blend	⊞
iShares S&P Europe 350 Index (IEV)	Europe Stock	⊞
iShares S&P MidCap 400/BARRA Growth (IJK)	Mid-Cap Growth	⊞
iShares MSCI Sweden Index (EWD)	Europe Stock	⊞
iShares Russell 3000 Value Index (IWW)	Large Value	⊞
iShares Dow Jones US Industrial (IYJ)	Large Blend	⊞
iShares S&P Global 100 Index (IOO)	World Stock	⊞
iShares MSCI Switzerland Index (EWL)	Europe Stock	⊞
iShares MSCI France Index (EWQ)	Europe Stock	⊞
Internet Architecture HOLDRs (IAH)	Specialty-Technology	⊞
Treasury 10 FITR ETF (TTE)	Intermediate Government	---
iShares MorningStar Large Core Index (JKD)	Large Blend	---
iShares S&P Global Healthcare Sector (IXJ)	Specialty-Health	⊞
iShares MSCI Pacific ex-Japan (EPP)	Pacific/Asia ex-Japan Stk	⊞
iShares MSCI Netherlands Index (EWN)	Europe Stock	⊞
iShares MSCI EMU Index (EZU)	Europe Stock	⊞
iShares Dow Jones US Financial Sector (IYF)	Specialty-Financial	⊞
iShares MSCI Spain Index (EWP)	Europe Stock	⊞
iShares Goldman Sachs Natural Resourc (IGE)	Specialty-Natural Res	⊞
Vanguard Extended Market Index VIPERs (VXF)	Mid-Cap Blend	---
Treasury 5 FITR ETF (TFI)	Short Government	---
Vanguard Health Care VIPERs (VHT)	Specialty-Health	---

Fund	Category	
iShares MorningStar Small Value Index (JKL)	Small Value	---
iShares MorningStar Large Value Index (JKF)	Large Value	---
Vanguard Value VIPERs (VTV)	Large Value	
Fortune 500 Index (FFF)	Large Growth	
iShares S&P Global Technology Sector (IXN)	Specialty-Technology	
iShares S&P Latin America 40 Index (ILF)	Latin America Stock	
streetTRACKS Wilshire REIT Fund (RWR)	Specialty-Real Estate	
iShares MorningStar Mid Value Index (JKI)	Mid-Cap Value	---
Vanguard Information Technology VIPERs (VGT)	Specialty-Technology	---
iShares MSCI Belgium Index (EWK)	Europe Stock	
iShares Dow Jones US Financial Svcs (IYG)	Specialty-Financial	
iShares MSCI Italy Index (EWI)	Europe Stock	
Powershares Dynamic OTC (PWO)	Large Value	
Vanguard Large Cap VIPERs (VV)	Large Blend	---
iShares S&P 1500 Index (ISI)	Large Blend	---
iShares MorningStar Small Core Index (JKJ)	Small Blend	---
BLDRS Asia 50 ADR Index (ADRA)	Diversified Pacific/Asia	
iShares S&P/TOPIX 150 Index (ITF)	Japan Stock	
iShares MorningStar Large Growth Index (JKE)	Large Growth	---
Vanguard Consumer Staples VIPERs (VDC)	Large Blend	---
Vanguard Financials VIPERs (VFH)	Specialty-Financial	---
streetTRACKS Morgan Stanley Technology (MTK)	Specialty-Technology	
iShares MorningStar Mid Core Index (JKG)	Mid-Cap Blend	---
streetTRACKS DJ Global Titans (DGT)	Large Blend	
streetTRACKS DJ US Small Cap Value (DSV)	Small Value	
iShares S&P Global Telecommunications (IXP)	Specialty-Communications	
Vanguard Growth VIPERs (VUG)	Large Growth	
iShares S&P Global Financials Sector (IXG)	Specialty-Financial	
iShares MSCI South Africa Index (EZA)	Foreign Large Blend	
Vanguard Consumer Discretionary VIPERs (VCR)	Large Blend	---
iShares MorningStar Small Growth Index (JKK)	Small Growth	---

Fresco Dow Jones STOXX 50 (FEU)	Europe Stock	▦
BLDRS Europe 100 ADR Index (ADRU)	Europe Stock	▦
Vanguard Small Cap VIPERs (VB)	Small Blend	▦
iShares MorningStar Mid Growth Index (JKH)	Mid-Cap Growth	---
Treasury 1 FITR ETF (TFT)	Short Government	---
Vanguard Materials VIPERs (VAW)	Specialty-Natural Res	---
BLDRS Emerging Markets 50 ADR Index (ADRE)	Diversified Emerging Mkts	▦
BLDRS Developed Markets 100 ADR Index (ADRD)	Foreign Large Blend	▦
Vanguard Utilities VIPERs (VPU)	Specialty-Utilities	---
Treasury 2 FITR ETF (TOU)	Short Government	---
Vanguard Mid Cap VIPERs (VO)	Mid-Cap Blend	▦
Vanguard Industrials VIPERs (VIS)		---

Notes

Other Works By Samuel Blankson

How to Destroy Your Debts

Printed: 165 pages, 6.0 x 9.0 in, Perfect-bound
Download: PDF (1739 kb)
ISBN: 1-4116-2374-6
Copyright Year: © 2005 by Samuel Blankson
Language: English
Publisher: Lulu.com

If you are like me, you hate being in debt! Every month you watch, your money run out before the end of the month. You scrape around for fuel and grocery money, and then finally you hit the credit cards, hoping they hold sufficient funds. If you want to get out of this cycle of worry over debt, this book may be your answer. I say, "May," because although this book will definitely give you techniques for controlling, managing, and even getting out of debt altogether, it will not do the work for you. That will be up to you. This book will reveal how to destroy your debts, including your mortgage. It will also make clear to you how you can increase your income, and have confidence in your financial future. Your journey to financial freedom begins here.

The Practical Guide to Total Financial Freedom: Volume 1

Printed: 124 pages, 8.5 x 11.0 in, Perfect-bound
Download: PDF (7761 kb)
ISBN: 1-4116-2058-5
Copyright Year: © 2005 by Samuel Blankson
Language: English
Publisher: Lulu.com

The first part of a five volume series on creating Total Financial Freedom. In this volume, you will learn the foundations of wealth building, and how to secure your family and your wealth against disasters and losses. This series offers practical, effective, and easy to follow advice for securely and quickly building wealth. If you are thinking of buying this book, you probably want to be free. Free from the rat race, free from the boss, free from the wage trap, and free from the mediocrity and hopelessness of poverty and lack of options. Until now, you may have had no other way of achieving this within the next half a decade. This book will change all that forever. This book, unlike many self-help books out there, will actually tell you what to do in order to achieve Total Financial Freedom. You will find out exactly how I went about achieving Total Financial Freedom. If you read, learn, and apply the lessons in this book, you too will achieve Total Financial Freedom.

The Practical Guide to Total Financial Freedom: Volume 2

Printed: 173 pages, 8.5 x 11.0 in, Perfect-bound
Download: PDF (31040 kb)
ISBN: 1-4116-2057-7
Copyright Year: © 2005 by Samuel Blankson
Language: English
Publisher: Lulu.com

The second part of a five volume series on creating Total Financial Freedom. In this volume, you will learn how to invest in Bonds, Stocks and Shares, and Funds. This series offers practical, effective, and easy to follow advice for securely and quickly building wealth. If you are thinking of buying this book, you probably want to be free. Free from the rat race, free from the boss, free from the wage trap, and free from the mediocrity and hopelessness of poverty and lack of options. Until now, you may have had no other way of achieving this within the next half a decade. This book will change all that forever. This book, unlike many self-help books out there, will actually tell you what to do in order to achieve Total Financial Freedom. You will find out exactly how I went about achieving Total Financial Freedom. If you read, learn, and apply the lessons in this book, you too will achieve Total Financial Freedom.

The Practical Guide to Total Financial Freedom: Volume 3

Printed: 143 pages, 8.5 x 11.0 in, Perfect-bound
Download: PDF (1716 kb)
ISBN: 1-4116-2056-9
Copyright Year: © 2005 by Samuel Blankson
Language: English
Publisher: Lulu.com

The third part of a five volume series on creating Total Financial Freedom. In this volume, you will learn how to invest in En Primeur Wine, Real Estate, Businesses, Life Insurances, Art, and Offshore investment opportunities. This series offers practical, effective, and easy to follow advice for securely and quickly building wealth. If you are thinking of buying this book, you probably want to be free. Free from the rat race, free from the boss, free from the wage trap, and free from the mediocrity and hopelessness of poverty and lack of options. Until now, you may have had no other way of achieving this within the next half a decade. This book will change all that forever. This book, unlike many self-help books out there, will actually tell you what to do in order to achieve Total Financial Freedom. You will find out exactly how I went about achieving Total Financial Freedom. If you read, learn, and apply the lessons in this book, you too will achieve Total Financial Freedom.

The Practical Guide to Total Financial Freedom: Volume 4

Printed: 134 pages, 8.5 x 11.0 in, Perfect-bound
Download: PDF (3961 kb)
ISBN: 1-4116-2055-0
Copyright Year: © 2005 by Samuel Blankson
Language: English
Publisher: Lulu.com

The fourth part of a five volume series on creating Total Financial Freedom. In this volume, you will learn how to trade and invest in Momentum products. These instruments are high-risk products that offer high returns, but also the possibilities of high losses. You will learn how to limit those losses by reducing the risk using effective and practical methods. Options, Futures, High Yield Investment Programs, and Gambling are some of the exciting topics covered in detail. This series offers practical, effective, and easy to follow advice for securely and quickly building wealth. This book, unlike many self-help books out there, will actually tell you what to do in order to achieve Total Financial Freedom. You will find out exactly how I went about achieving Total Financial Freedom. If you read, learn, and apply the lessons in this book, you too will achieve Total Financial Freedom.

The Practical Guide to Total Financial Freedom: Volume 5

Printed: 322 pages, 8.5 x 11.0 in, Perfect-bound
Download: PDF (7143 kb)
ISBN: 1-4116-2054-2
Copyright Year: © 2005 by Samuel Blankson
Language: English
Publisher: Lulu.com

The last part of a five volume series on creating Total Financial Freedom. In this volume, you will learn how to lower your taxes, avoid paying unfair and unnecessary taxes, and how to move offshore and pay no taxes at all. This series offers practical, effective, and easy to follow advice for securely and quickly building wealth. If you are thinking of buying this book, you probably want to be free. Free from the rat race, free from the boss, free from the wage trap, and free from the mediocrity and hopelessness of poverty and lack of options. Until now, you may have had no other way of achieving this within the next half a decade. This book will change all that forever. This book, unlike many self-help books out there, will actually tell you what to do in order to achieve Total Financial Freedom. You will find out exactly how I went about achieving Total Financial Freedom. If you read, learn, and apply the lessons in this book, you too will achieve Total Financial Freedom.

Living the Ultimate Truth, 2nd Edition

Printed: 166 pages, 6.0 x 9.0 in, Perfect-bound
Download: PDF (855 kb)
ISBN: 1-4116-2375-4
Copyright Year: © 2005 by Samuel Blankson
Language: English
Publisher: Lulu.com

Today most people live a poor example of a balanced life. The centuries of wisdom passed down from the great leaders of our past seem lost amid lives centred on minutia and selfishness. Today we care more about what we wear and where we are seen, than we do about discovering and Living the Ultimate Truth. Throughout the world, there is an imbalance in people's spirituality, consciousness, and inner harmony. This has taken a great toll on our environment, our health, and our happiness. Many are wondering around like lost sheep, seeking a shepherd in all the wrong places. Many false prophets have promised quick fixes to these problems, but if these solutions are not firmly rooted in The Creator, love, integrity and inner harmony, they are doomed to fail. This book is a reminder of all those virtues and universal principles that we need, to return to a balanced, harmonious, and happy life. You will learn to love yourself, love others, and finally find that inner peace you seek through spiritual growth.

Developing Personal Integrity, 2nd Edition

Printed: 118 pages, 6.0 x 9.0 in, Perfect-bound
Download: PDF (627 kb)
ISBN: 1-4116-2376-2
Copyright Year: © 2005 by Samuel Blankson
Language: English
Publisher: Lulu.com

In the field of human character development, integrity is the last frontier. Many people use the word, but few really know what real integrity is. This book breaks down the fundamental components of personal integrity and offers a path to attaining it. Like success or happiness, integrity is a journey not a destination. We can only measure how far on the path we are through the observation of our inner voice, the voice of our conscience, and through deep contemplation and reflection. This journey of personal excellence is not an easy one, and as a friend once said, "When peeling this onion, sometimes you cry." Nevertheless, in all great endeavours, the harder the struggle, the greater the victory will be.

The Guide to Real Estate Investing

Printed: 117 pages, 6.0 x 9.0 in, Perfect-bound
Download: PDF (723 kb)
ISBN: 1-4116-2383-5
Copyright Year: © 2005 by Samuel Blankson
Language: English
Publisher: Lulu.com

If you have ever wanted to know how to make money from real estate, but could never find one source that listed and explained all the different options available to you, then your search is over. This book covers over 20 different ways of investing in real estate. You will find the author's style easy to understand and very practical. The section on self-build is so in-depth, that after reading it you will actually know how to build a house, and the section on REITs, Indexes, and REIT Options will leave your mind boggling at the potential profits available to you. This book also covers the conversional and popular methods of real estate investing as well. Therefore, whether you want to learn to develop real estate projects, build your own home, or simply rent a room in your house, this book will help you maximise your success and avoid the pitfalls.

Making Money with Funds

Printed: 79 pages, 6.0 x 9.0 in., Perfect-bound
Download: PDF (8769 kb)
ISBN: 1-4116-2671-0
Copyright Year: © 2005 by Samuel Blankson
Language: English
Publisher: Lulu.com

Today the world fund market is a multi trillion-dollar industry. There are many types of funds and as many reasons for choosing them. In this book, you will learn how Funds work, and how you, can make money with them.

How to make a fortune with Options trading

Printed: 59 pages, 8.5 x 11.0 in, Perfect-bound
Download: PDF (1808 kb)
ISBN: 1-4116-2378-9
Copyright Year: © 2005 by Samuel Blankson
Language: English
Publisher: Lulu.com

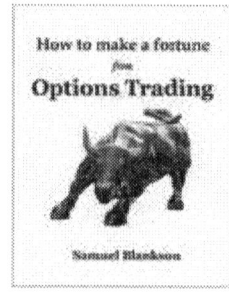

This is a practical book on winning in the Options trading market. Whether you are a sophisticated investor or a complete novice, this book is for you. The author takes complex ideas, and explains them in a way that is both practical and easily understood by anyone. Having used these techniques to achieve financial freedom, Mr Blankson now shares with you how he did it. There is no waffling here, just plain speaking and powerful techniques that anyone can apply.

How to make a fortune on the Stock Markets

Printed: 190 pages, 8.5 x 11.0 in, Perfect-bound
Download: PDF (8769 kb)
ISBN: 1-4116-2379-7
Copyright Year: © 2005 by Samuel Blankson
Language: English
Publisher: Lulu.com

This book contains simple but effective techniques for achieving regular and consistent profits from stock trading. Unlike other books on the topic, it is not full of theory and projections, but practical advice learned the hard way, by trading personal hard-earned cash daily in the world's stock exchanges. Moreover, unlike other books on the subject, it is not about how to be a stock trader and trade other people's money, but on how to grow your own funds to a level where you will never have to work for anyone else again. This book contains real techniques used by the author to amass a fortune significant enough to have made him Financially Free. Now you too can use these simple but highly effective techniques to achieve the same results. Therefore, whether you are a professional trader or a total beginner, this book will show you how to achieve Financial Freedom through trading Stocks and Shares.

Tax Avoidance A practical guide for UK Residents

Printed: 104 pages, 6.0 x 9.0 in, Perfect-bound
Download: PDF (355 kb)
ISBN: 1-4116-2380-0
Copyright Year: © 2005 by Samuel Blankson
Language: English
Publisher: Lulu.com

UK residents pay some of the highest taxes in the world. Most of these taxes are hidden through VAT and service charges. This guide clearly explains what taxes you are paying, and which ones you can and should avoid paying through claiming your allowed deductions and allowances. Prudent tax efficient estate planning is explained in detail, and hundreds of tax saving ideas are shared within these pages. Whether you are a qualified accountant or a non-professional, you will find this little guide an invaluable source of tax saving ideas and strategies.

The Ultimate Guide to Offshore Tax Havens

Printed: 418 pages, 8.5 x 11.0 in, Perfect-bound
Download: PDF (12602 kb)
ISBN: 1-4116-2384-3
Copyright Year: © 2005 by Samuel Blankson
Language: English
Publisher: Lulu.com

This book is a detailed listing of all the known and not so commonly known Tax Havens, their benefits, and their suitability for relocation by the low tax seeker. If you are looking for ways to cut your taxes, there is no better way than to relocate to a low or no tax haven. The South East Asian Tsunamis and earthquakes have shown us that it is prudent to select the haven you will reside in carefully. Low taxes cannot be your only gauge for this task. This book will help you make that decision.

A must read for all who aspire to changing their lifestyles by relocating offshore. The havens are listed in geographical order, starting with the USA and ending with the South Pacific Islands.

Attitude

Printed: 418 pages, 6.0 x 9.0 in, Perfect-bound
Download: PDF (13700 kb)
ISBN: 1-4116-2382-7
Copyright Year: © 2005 by Samuel Blankson
Language: English
Publisher: Lulu.com

Attitude, so often misunderstood, yet so vital for success in every aspect of our lives. A positive attitude will guarantee happiness in your life, promotion and growth in your career or job, peace and joy in your family life, and in addition, a positive attitude has been scientifically proven to help extend your life expectancy. In this book, this essential success attribute is explained in detail. You will learn how to safeguard against positive attitude erosion, and learn how to build a positive mental attitude to help you achieve measurable success in every aspect of your life.

How to win at Greyhound betting

Printed: 68 pages, 8.5 x 11.0 in, Perfect-bound
Download: PDF (639 kb)
ISBN: 1-4116-2377-0
Copyright Year: © 2005 by Samuel Blankson
Language: English
Publisher: Lulu.com

Today, sports betting is a big industry for the bookmakers and organisers. Of all the people who benefit from sports racing, the "punters" (or in this case, you), are the last on the list of people who consistently gain. In fact, the greyhounds probably gain more from these races than most punters. Why is that? Well, there are many reasons, but most of them centre on these two things: lack of a proven system, and greed. This book closely examines these two points, and offers techniques and systems for achieving consistent wins in greyhound betting.

The Ultimate Greyhound Betting System

Download: MS Excel (233 kb)
Copyright Year: © 2005 by Samuel
Blankson
Language: English
Publisher: Lulu.com

If you think there is no trustworthy betting system out there, then prepare to be proven wrong. This is the betting system described in the series *The Practical Guide to Total Financial Freedom,* and the book *How to win at Greyhound betting.* This semi-automatic system allows its user to achieve a minimum of 30% profits per week by following a proven statistical and rule based system betting on UK Greyhound races. The system only requires you to supply the race results and place the bets with your bookmaker. Armed with this incredible system, you will be able to beat the odds, and win one over the bookmakers.

How to Win at Online Roulette

Printed: 81 pages, 6.0 x 9.0 in, Perfect-bound
ISBN: 1-4116-2570-6
Copyright Year: © 2005 by Samuel
Blankson
Language: English
Publisher: Lulu.com

This is a guide to consistently winning at online Roulette. It is a simple and to the point writing about an amazing system for gaining an advantage at online Casinos. This book will show you how to make £1000 per day or more from online Roulette.

Sixty Original Song Lyrics

Printed: 200 pages, 6.0 x 9.0 in, Perfect-bound
Download: PDF (1072 kb)
ISBN: 1-4116-2059-3
Copyright Year: © 2004 by Samuel Blankson
Language: English
Publisher: Lulu.com

This is a compilation of original song lyrics by Samuel Blankson. This book contains 60 of the songs he wrote in between 2000 – 2002. Having had some of these lyrics made into songs for an album (see *www.practicalbooks.org*), and several of them now on compilations, Samuel now shares these 60 song lyrics with you.

Images of Kilimanjaro

Printed: 53 pages, 8.5 x 11.0 in, Perfect-bound
Download: PDF (2573 kb)
ISBN: 1-4116-2016-X
Copyright Year: © 2004
Language: English
Publisher: Lulu.com

This is a book of pictures taken from Kilimanjaro. This is an accompanying book to the Calendar of the same name.

Images of Kilimanjaro

Printed: 26 pages, 11 x 8.5 in, Coil-bound
Start Date: January 1st, 2006
Duration: 12 months
Copyright Year: © 2004 by Samuel Blankson
Language: English
Publisher: Lulu.com

Kilimanjaro, the tallest freestanding mountain in the world, is captured here for you to feast your eyes on each month through 2006. Kilimanjaro is a source of life for Tanzania and Kenya locals, who live on its life giving rains and water. I had the honour of climbing this majestic mountain, and captured the essence of its allure and mystery through these pictures.

Uju

Download: MPG (6523 kb)
UPC: 4-3157-3526-2
Copyright Year: © 2004 by Samuel and Uju Blankson
Language: English
Publisher: Lulu.com

A six track EP with soulful R&B tracks with a pop flavour. This EP is bound to have you humming along addictively. For more info about the artist Uju, visit *www.uju-music.com* and look out for her forthcoming album.

The Bass by Samuel Blankson

Download: MPG (4811 kb)
Copyright Year: © 2004 by Samuel and
Uju Blankson
Language: English
Publisher: Lulu.com

A sexy, R&B track with wicked beats and a deep baseline. With a melody and chorus that will stay with you for a long time, this addictive and catchy tune deserves your download (see *www.practicalbooks.org*).

Investing in En Primeur Wine

Printed: 88 pages, 6.0 x 9.0 in, Perfect-bound
Download: PDF (1,095 kb)
ISBN: 1-4116-2867-5
Copyright Year: © 2005
Language: English
Publisher: Lulu.com

Wine investing is not new, it has been going on for centuries. In more recent years (the last two centuries), government tax laws on alcoholic drinks have made buying wine a little more prohibitive to the investor who wants to keep them at home in his/her private cellar. Nevertheless, as usual, the market has found a way around this problem.

You can avoid taxes and V.A.T. (Value Added Tax) by buying fine wine on Bond (also called wine Futures or En Primeur). This book covers a simple and effective way in which anybody coming into the fine wine investing market place can safely securely and successfully select, and invest in En Primeur Wine.

Eight Steps to Success

Printed: 105 pages, 6.0 x 9.0 in, Perfect-bound
Download: PDF (1,095 kb)
ISBN: 1-4116-2738-5
Copyright Year: © 2005
Language: English
Publisher: Lulu.com

We would all like to live a successful life, a life where our relationships and finances are a source of happiness and joy. This life is attainable by following timeless success principles. These principles have been forgotten by our fast food, fast-paced, reality TV society.

This book defines, explains, and shows you how to apply these principles and skills in your life to attain happiness, contentment, peace, joy, and prosperity. The eight fundamental virtues and skills required to succeed long-term in any endeavour, are explained in detail and in a style that everyone can understand and immediately apply.

The Eight Steps to Success is an inspirational book that will help you understand, acquire, hone, and apply the principles of success.

Taking Action

Printed: 105 pages, 6.0 x 9.0 in, Perfect-bound
Download: PDF (1,095 kb)
ISBN: 1-4116-2735-0
Copyright Year: © 2005
Language: English
Publisher: Lulu.com

This is a book about taking action. For some, taking action means something you will do, might do, should do, have done, or never will do. This book will show you how to change your understanding of taking action to mean something you are doing NOW! When you change this focus in your life, you will release great powers. This book will show you how to tap into this phenomenal power and change your life.

About The Author

An entrepreneur at heart, Samuel Blankson blends art, creativity, passion, business acumen, and financial expertise with careful planning and execution in the achievement of measurable results. He is an avid reader, writer, researcher, and securities trader.

He is an advocate of self-empowerment and an individual's ability to control their destiny through the achievement of personal freedom from economic, financial, spiritual, social, mental, and interrelationship restrictions. Samuel is constantly working to push the boundaries of personal achievements to their limits, recognising that these limits are only self-imposed.

Samuel has authored over twenty books (*How to Destroy Your Debts*, *Living the Ultimate Truth*, *Developing Personal Integrity*, *The Practical Guide to Total Financial Freedom* volumes 1, 2, 3, 4 and 5, and *Attitude* are some of these works). He has written over 100 songs, sixty of which are featured in *Sixty Original Song Lyrics*. He writes poetry, creates artwork, and works daily to express his creativity in many ways.

Having successfully run several businesses, Samuel diversified into securities trading over a decade ago, with great success. After learning from the masters of the time, Samuel progressed to develop his own methods and systems for successful trading. Today, he trades many financial instruments and has developed ways of successfully generating profits from his many investments.

A firm believer in knowledge sharing, Samuel travels the globe, teaching and sharing his personal knowledge with groups of friends, associates, and anyone who seeks to improve their life. This is the spirit of Samuel Blankson, a God centred philanthropist, overcomer, and high achiever.

www.ingramcontent.com/pod-product-compliance
Lightning Source LLC
Chambersburg PA
CBHW022104170526
45157CB00004B/1473